A Journey
INTO Reality

lessons from Genesis

Silas Martin
with Joel Erickson

A Journey into Reality: Lessons from Genesis

Milestone Books
34207 Enos Drive
Halsey, OR 97348
800-761-0234
office@milestonebooks.com

ISBN: 978-0-692-41995-3

First printing: May 2015

Printed in the United States of America.

All scripture quotations are taken from the King James Version.

To the rising generations

that they might find
reality in God and in all His works

by which they can avoid
the vain philosophies of men
who are ever learning
but never able to come to
the knowledge of the truth

Contents

Acknowledgments

To the Lord my God: for putting in my heart the vision for this work, knowing full well my inability to accomplish it alone. I recognize this is the way You often work. Thank You for supplying other helpers and encouragers so the work could go on. Use it to magnify Your Name.

To my friends Donald and Donna Chittick: for your support and encouragement from the very beginning. Without you, this book would have never come about. I am deeply indebted for the many hours you spent going over my rough manuscripts. Thank you for your comments and corrections, especially those related to biblical and scientific facts. You enlarged my vision. May God bless you richly for your labor of love. It has been a joy to work with you.

To my coauthor and editor Joel Erickson: for taking my rough manuscripts and polishing them, adding many interesting details, which would have been impossible for me to do. Thank you for designing the book and seeing the project through to publication. In some ways it is more your work than mine. I am exceedingly grateful.

To my crew of reviewers: for taking time from your busy schedules and giving me your comments and criticism. Your input has been valuable.

To my dear wife, Martha Ruth Martin, my help meet of 58 years, and the mother of our six children: for sustaining me and encouraging me in the work, especially in my declining health. You have been such a blessing.

And now it is a great joy to present this work to the rising generation. It is my desire that you also will set your hope in God. Life is a journey, and the Bible is a precious guide. It would be a joy to meet each of you in heaven in the ages to come.

Silas Martin
April 2015

Introduction

"What is truth?" This question that Pilate asked Jesus has echoed in the hearts of men all through the ages, and is as fresh today as ever. Surely life is more than mere existence. Who has the answers? How can we discern what is right among so many competing claims?

What we find will depend on how much we really want to know. Pilate asked in unbelief—and went on his way no nearer the answer than before. But when Thomas asked, "How can we know the way?" he really meant it. The answer Jesus gave was simple, yet it deserves our complete attention: *"I am the way, the truth, and the life"* (John 14:6).

There are right answers to life's questions, and they can be found if we search with all our heart. The purpose of this book is to aid you in the search for truth, for reality. The witness of creation surrounds us every day. Life abounds on every hand, waiting for us to hear its story. Furthermore, the Creator has given us a record of His creative work, telling us why things are the way they are. There is much we do not know, but by studying the works of God and comparing it with the Word from God, we can discover the Way, the Truth, and the Life. We can come to know the "I AM."

Of all the forms of life that God has created, only the human family was granted the gift of conscious thought. This special gift from our Creator makes it possible to communicate our thoughts with one another and with Him. Also, we have been given the freedom to make our own choices in life. But with freedom comes responsibility. We are accountable to God for the choices we make, so it is very important that we make right choices.

Since we are on a Journey into Reality, we will discover that what men believe about things and how they really are do not always agree. In fact, men often disagree with one another, coming to different conclusions. Consider, for example, the field of cosmology. Throughout the ages men have studied the stars and tried to understand their movements. Even today our government spends billions of dollars to explore the heavens.

Currently, there are two basic schools of thought on how the solar system works. In the heliocentric model, the sun is at the center, and the earth goes around it once a year. This is the model commonly taught in textbooks. In the other, the geocentric model, the earth is at rest at the center of the universe, and the heavenly bodies move around it. That the sun, moon, and stars are up there is reality, but what men believe about them is another matter. Since new discoveries are constantly being made, scientific notions come and go.

What is the "glue" that holds the universe together, causing it to run like clockwork year after year, century after century? The Bible tells us simply that Jesus upholds all things by the word of His power—the same word and power that set it all in motion at the very beginning of time (Hebrews 1:2-3). Since the Bible consistently portrays a moving sun and the earth at rest, just as we observe, in this book I have made no effort to conform to the ever-changing winds of scientific models.

Science can be defined as the knowledge gained through study of the natural world. If we look fairly at this knowledge, we will find that it speaks clearly of a supernatural source—our Creator. He has not been silent on the subject, and I invite you to join me as we explore the tremendous significance of this reality.

> *To the only wise God our Saviour, be glory and majesty, dominion and power, both now and ever. Amen.* (Jude 25)

A Journey INTO Reality

lessons from Genesis

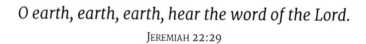

O earth, earth, earth, hear the word of the Lord.

JEREMIAH 22:29

A Journey into Reality

As we grow up, we begin to seek answers to some very important questions. How did the world and everything in it get here? Where did life come from? Why am I here? Why is there evil in the world, and why do bad things happen? Does it matter how I live?

People will give us many different answers to these questions. But how can we know which answers are right? We know that the correct answers will agree with reality, that is, the way things really are.

Picture in your mind two people standing on the rim of the Grand Canyon. They can both gaze for hours at the scene before them. What they see is reality. Based on what they believe, they may each come to quite different conclusions about what they see, but what they believe does not change the canyon.

People all around the world can look up and observe the sun, moon, and stars. They are real. What people believe about them may be quite different. Some try to explain what makes them move. Others may even worship them. But all the ideas about these objects in the sky do not change reality. They are there day after day. That is reality. Reality cannot be changed by human thought.

Life presents one of the most challenging questions of all. There may be millions of living things, from the smallest germ to the largest tree. There is also sea life, bird life, other animal life, and human life, in what seems endless variety. But each kind of life reproduces the same kind. And each kind of life we see today has continued from generation to generation since the beginning. So then we wonder, what was the first of each kind that began each of these life chains? Again, people come up with different ideas. But life is real. We see evidence of it everywhere. What people believe about life and where it comes from does not change the facts. Life exists! Reality is what is.

Most importantly, we can know the truth about life and reality. When we see a house, we know someone built it. That is reality. When we see living things, we know that there had to be a beginning. Things don't "just happen," even in a billion years. That is reality. Everything has a maker, or creator. When people make something to sell that is complicated, they often include an instruction manual on how to use it. Our Creator has also given us an instruction manual that tells us how the worlds were created and how to live here and why things are the way they are. We call this manual the Bible. The Bible records the important information from the beginning until the time of Jesus and the Apostles. Only our Creator knows the true story and the whole story.

We have two witnesses that help us answer life's basic questions: the created world, and the Bible. These two witnesses are in perfect agreement, because they come from the same source: the Creator. That is reality. People may disagree with their witness, but that does not change reality.

The scope of this study covers the first few chapters of the book of Genesis in the Bible. Journey with me as we look at our world from our Creator's vantage point.

God Wants Us to Know

Suppose you and your friends are going on a camping trip. It's a big deal because you'll need to pack all your gear and hike quite a way into the wilds. You're excited because you like to hike and you've heard great things about your destination. But since none of you has ever been there before, you'll want to make sure you get a map with good directions. Better yet would be to find someone who knows the trail well and would be willing to go along as your guide.

Life is like that. You have never traveled this way before. If you are going to arrive safely at your final campsite, you need direction. God has given you both a map and a guide. The Bible is your road map to show you the way. It also shows the many paths that would lead you astray. You can observe where these paths lead in the lives of the many people who have lived before you. If you take care to learn from the Bible, you can save yourself from many a wrong turn. God also sent His own son Jesus to live here and travel the trail too. There is no better guide. Many a misstep can be avoided if you follow Him, for He knows the way.

How did we get the Bible? When God created our world, He did not walk off and leave us to our own imagination. He gave us a record so we could know how and when the heavens and the earth were created. He wanted us to know who the first people were, and why there is evil in the world. And He wants us to understand why our world is the way it is today. If God had not given us a record, we would not know how we got here or why we are here. It is the Bible that gives us the important answers we need to understand life. Science has given us many useful things to use and enjoy, but science cannot give us the real answers about the meaning and purpose of life.

Did God actually write the Bible? The books of the Bible—which are also called the Scriptures—were written by men, but God put into their minds what they should write. So we say that God inspired the Bible, and we call it God's Word. *"Knowing this first, that no prophecy of the scripture is of any private interpretation. For the prophecy came not in old time by the will of man: but holy men of God spake as they were moved by the Holy Ghost"* (2 Peter 1:20-21). *"All scripture is given by inspiration of God, and is profitable for doctrine, for reproof, for correction, for instruction in righteousness"* (2 Timothy 3:16). The Bible tells us what we need to know in order to live a worthy, useful life that is pleasing to our Creator. God is good.

Your Bible is God's precious gift to you. If you believe the Bible and obey what it teaches, you will have wisdom from God in your hands and heart and you will know how to live in a right way. People who do not believe what God tells us in the Bible try to figure out life for themselves. But they can never really know the truth, because God's Word tells us the truth, and they don't believe God. Some who think they are very wise tell us things that are not according to God's Word, and try to convince us they are true. But because they do not believe God, we cannot believe them, because God tells us the truth. He does not lie! The Bible tells us all the important things we really need to know.

The very first thing that the Bible tells us is, *"In the beginning God created the heaven and the earth."* Some people don't believe that. They think our world got here by chance. They have some very strange ideas, and they keep changing their minds from time to time. But think about it: if you have a bicycle, you know someone made it. If you live in a house, you know someone built it. You know someone made your clothes. Things do not just happen all by themselves. So we know our world is here because someone made it. And the Bible tells us that

4

"someone" is God. Only God could make a sunset. Only God could make a tree. Only God could make a human body like He gave you and me.

The Bible also tells us why there are bad things in this world. It tells us why people hate, and kill, and do many sinful things. It tells us about Satan and his evil doings. It even tells us why we do bad things as well. But the Bible also tells us that God sent His Son Jesus into the world so that by believing in Him we can be saved from sin. While Jesus was here He taught us the right way to live, and did many kind and wonderful things to help needy people. In the end He gave Himself to die on the cross so that we could be saved and go to heaven to be with God forever. The Bible is the most wonderful book. Not only does it show us the way God wants us to live, but it also tells how He will help us live that way.

You see, God wants us to know these things, and much, much more. That is why He gave us the Bible. He did not want us to try to figure it out for ourselves, for we would not be able to get it right without His help. God does not want us to be ignorant of the many things we need to know. Sometimes we may read things in the Bible that we do not understand. We might not know how it could be true, but that simply means that we lack understanding. So don't be discouraged. Start with what you are able to understand, and God will help you understand more and more as you grow older. For some things, we'll just have to wait until we get to heaven to understand them. But because God has told us many things in the Bible, we can know that He loves us very much and that He wants us to be with Him in heaven for all eternity.

In the Beginning

Sometimes we say that God is eternal. We might call God the Eternal God. Eternal means without beginning and without end. Our small minds cannot understand that. When Moses asked God what he should tell the people if they asked who sent him, God gave him this response to say: *"I AM hath sent me unto you"* (Exodus 3:14). God is the only "I AM"—God IS! When God created the heavens and the earth, He also created time. We think of past, present, and future, but God is eternal. When Genesis 1:1 says, *"In the beginning,"* it is talking about when God began creating our world. This was the starting point He gave us.

God created the heavens and the earth by His spoken word. When you read Genesis 1 you will notice that *"And God said"* is recorded again and again. Count and see how often those words are repeated. This is how our world and the starry heavens came to be. Look outside and see all the wonderful things God has created. Our God is a marvelous Creator.

The earth was not made out of something which existed before (Hebrew 11:3). It was a brand new creation to provide a home for people. God also planned that if people would choose to believe and obey Him, then He would then take them to heaven to live with Him there forever. God has placed us here so we could choose to love and obey Him.

God created the heavens and the earth about 6000 years ago. How do we know? The Bible gives a lot of exact dates and times when things happened. For example, *"Adam lived an hundred and thirty years, and begat a son... and called his name Seth"* (Genesis 5:3). *"And Seth lived an hundred and five years and begat Enos"* (vs. 6). *"And Enos lived ninety years and begat Cainan"* (vs. 9). Read all of Genesis 5 and it will bring you right up the time of Noah, who built the ark. There are many such places in the Bible that help us put together the chain of times and dates when things happened. As a result, it is possible to determine about how many years ago the world was created.

Many years ago a man named James Ussher (1581–1656) made a detailed study of the chronological information that is recorded in the Bible. He was a very exacting and careful student. This is what he concluded: "The beginning of time, according to our chronology, happened at the start of the evening preceding the 23rd day of October (on the Julian calendar), 4004 BC.... (This day was the first Sunday past the autumnal equinox for that year....)" God began to create on day number one, and on our calendar the first day of the week is Sunday. It is true that God has not given us every detail, so several assumptions must be made to conclude on a precise date. Others have done calculations as well and have come up with slightly different figures, but there is not much difference in their conclusions. So we can confidently say that the world is about 6000 years old. We can also calculate fairly accurately when the Great Flood occurred. God chose to place this information in the Bible so we can know and not be deceived by unbelievers who tell us the world is millions or billions of years old. That claim simply is not true.

The beginning in Genesis 1 was the beginning of time. This is when days, weeks, months and years began. We continue to follow that pattern today. God has a plan and purpose in everything that He does and in His wisdom set all these things in order for us. Oh, the wisdom and love of God for us! He did these things for our first parents, Adam and Eve, and for all the people that followed after.

And now we are going to look more closely at the very first day.

The First Day: Light and Time

¹In the beginning God created the heaven and the earth.

This simple sentence introduces us to God's creative work. If that was all He told us, it would be enough for us to understand, but He wanted us to know some details of how He went about it. God could have created the world and all things in it with one word, but instead He chose to do it over six days, one part at a time. The six creation days, plus the seventh day when He rested, established the first week. If we study this chapter carefully we can learn many things about the earth on which we live and about our God who created it.

²And the earth was without form, and void; and darkness was upon the face of the deep. And the Spirit of God moved upon the face of the waters. ³And God said, Let there be light: and there was light. ⁴And God saw the light, that it was good: and God divided the light from the darkness. ⁵And God called the light Day, and the darkness he called Night. And the evening and the morning were the first day.

At first the earth was *"without form, and void."* This tells us it was not finished or complete. It was covered with water and everything was dark. Then, step by step, God transformed the earth into a beautiful home for the human family.

The Bible tells us that God is light (1 John 1:5). So what is the very first thing God said? *"Let there be light: and there was light."* Then God divided the light from the darkness, so that one part of the earth was light while the other side was dark. Since there was evening and morning it is reasonable to believe that the whole earth was not lighted at once, but this localized light moved around the earth, providing evening and morning all around the world, like we have today. While the Bible does not tell us where the light came from, it does say something very interesting. It tells us the Spirit of God was moving upon the face of the water, so that first light may have come directly from God's Spirit moving around the earth on the face of the waters. This would have set the pattern for the sun which God later created on the fourth day. If that were the case, then in every place around the earth there would have been evening and morning, just as Genesis tells us.

We must be careful when we study the Bible, and not call something a fact unless the Bible says it is. So we cannot say for sure that the evening and morning worked like described above, though it may seem a reasonable suggestion. We must not add to or subtract from God's word. God's word is pure, so we cannot improve upon it.

When God divided the light from the darkness, He named the light "day" and the darkness "night" (vs. 5). But more often when the word "day" is used, it includes the time of darkness. Did you notice that the Bible says, *"the evening and the morning were the first day"*? A day started in the evening and lasted until the next evening. The Jews and some other people still count a day in this manner. In America, a "civil day" is measured from midnight to midnight, like the Romans did, yet we usually think of the day as beginning in the morning when it gets light.

We divide our days into 24 hours of equal length. This is helpful, since most people now have consistent clocks to measure with, and we like to be able to work with exact times of the day for business and other activities. But because most people the Bible mentions in early times were farmers, raising crops and animals, this was not so important, and they didn't count by hours like we do. People measured time by the position of the sun, which changed according to the seasons. The time of day was usually mentioned as simply morning, noonday, and evening. Nighttime was divided into three "watches" for those who must be awake to guard animals or property.

Other cultures, such as the Babylonians and Romans, were interested in measuring the time of day more precisely. So by the time of the New Testament, when the Jews were governed by the Romans, they were using hours to measure the daylight. And the night was divided into four watches that were each three hours long.

This chart compares how time was measured in the Bible and how it is measured today. It is only an approximate comparison, because the length of day and night are only about equal at the equator. The time of sunrise and sunset will be earlier or later depending on how far you live from the equator (latitude) and the season of the year.

Also, in Bible times, the hours of day were divided equally from sunrise to sunset. For example, in Jerusalem on winter solstice (the shortest day, usually December 21 or 22) sunrise is about 6:35 AM and sunset about 4:40 PM local time, so each hour would have been only 50 minutes long. On the longest day, the first day of summer, each hour would have been about 71 minutes long.

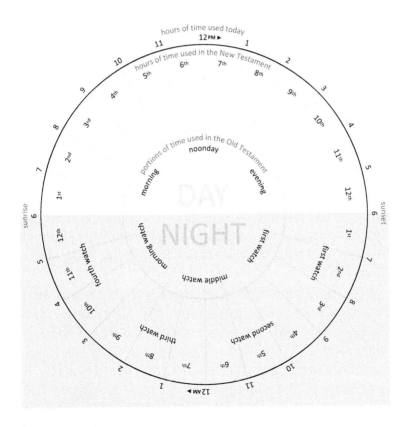

The Second Day: The Firmament

⁶And God said, Let there be a firmament in the midst of the waters, and let it divide the waters from the waters. ⁷And God made the firmament, and divided the waters which were under the firmament from the waters which were above the firmament: and it was so. ⁸And God called the firmament Heaven. And the evening and the morning were the second day.

Here God describes how He created the heavens. It is very easy to understand, once you have learned the word *firmament*. The dictionary says the firmament is the arch of the sky, and that is how it looks to us when we go outside and see it stretching from one horizon to the other. Yet it is much, much bigger than what we can see. No matter where you are on earth—whether you live in China, or Norway, or Argentina—you can look up and see a part of this amazing firmament. High above us we see the sun and moon make their daily journey around the earth. Here also we see the countless number of stars which God spread all across the sky. Children in the north learn to find the group of stars we call the Big Dipper. Down on the other side of the world these cannot be seen, but the children there can find the stars of the Southern Cross.

You will remember that when the earth was first created it was completely covered with deep water. Now we learn that God divided the waters and placed some of them above the firmament—or as we might say, above the sky. Some men think that the firmament or "universe" is infinite, meaning unlimited in size. But everything God created has limits, although we may never be able to measure them. The Bible likens the firmament to a tent or a tabernacle, indicating it has an outer covering or an outer limit, and the record in Genesis suggests that the outer limit was formed by water. According to the book of Psalms those waters are still up there. *"Praise him, ye heavens of heavens, and ye waters that be above the heavens"* (Psalm 148:4). Men with their most powerful telescopes have not yet discovered the waters above the firmament or the outer limit of the heavens.

Because the firmament is so very large, when we look up in the sky we can actually only see a very small part of it. Every time a bigger and more powerful telescope is invented, scientists discover more stars, planets, and other things that God put in outer space. Closer to us, we have the atmosphere of air that covers the earth. Although usually invisible, we can see clouds floating in it, and feel the breeze as it moves, and watch the beautiful colors of a sunset as the light shines through it. This layer of air in the firmament makes it possible for birds and planes to fly. And of course we must have air to breathe, as do many plants and animals. God also established the laws of gravity and motion and other forces that keep everything in order. As these forces work in the atmosphere and the rest of the firmament, they keep the air here on earth where we need it, they cause the rain to fall down instead of up, and they allow you to fly a kite or throw a ball. In fact, God has designed the firmament for so many marvelous things that we could spend our whole lives learning about them and still only know a little of it.

But God knows every inch, for He created the firmament for His glory and so that men can behold the wonderful works which He has made. You can go anywhere in the world and still see some part of the firmament, for God made it to surround the earth, which is the center of His creation. In Psalm 19 we read this beautiful description:

¹The heavens declare the glory of God; and the firmament sheweth his handywork. ²Day unto day uttereth speech, and night unto night sheweth knowledge. ³There is no speech nor language, where their voice is not heard. ⁴Their line is gone out through all the earth, and their words to the end of the world. In them hath he set a tabernacle for the sun, ⁵Which is as a bridegroom coming out of his chamber, and rejoiceth as a strong man to run a race. ⁶His going forth is from the end of the heaven, and his circuit unto the ends of it: and there is nothing hid from the heat thereof.

Why was God doing all these things? He was preparing a home for all the people that would live on the earth. It was perfectly designed to meet our every need so we could live happy and useful lives. We can be sure it did not happen by chance like some unbelievers tell us. That would be impossible. Our faithful and loving Creator made it for all the many living creatures that He created, but most of all for us. God loves us, and He desires to have a loving relationship with each of us.

The Third Day: Dry Ground and Plants

9And God said, Let the waters under the heaven be gathered together unto one place, and let the dry land appear: and it was so. 10And God called the dry land Earth; and the gathering together of the waters called he Seas: and God saw that it was good. 11And God said, Let the earth bring forth grass, the herb yielding seed, and the fruit tree yielding fruit after his kind, whose seed is in itself, upon the earth: and it was so. 12And the earth brought forth grass, and herb yielding seed after his kind, and the tree yielding fruit, whose seed was in itself, after his kind: and God saw that it was good. 13And the evening and the morning were the third day.

On this third day, God moved forward in preparing a home for mankind. Up to this time the earth had been completely covered with water, but now God gathered the waters together and caused dry land to appear. We like to name the things that we make, and God does too, so He named the waters "seas" and the dry land "earth." We use the word "earth" like that sometimes to describe only the dry ground, and sometimes to describe the whole world, even the parts under water. Today it is estimated that about 70% of the earth is covered with water. But back before the Flood changed everything, the shape of the land and sea as God first made it was probably very different.

After making the dry ground, God stopped to take a look at what He had done. When we look back over something we have worked on, we often find things that need to be fixed, but God always gets it right the first time. He never makes any mistakes. God saw that the dry ground was good. It was just what He needed for what He was going to do next.

What God did next was to cover the ground with grass, herbs, and trees—the very first living things. When first created, many of these plants were already in full maturity. The herbs had seed and the trees had fruit. Each was designed to reproduce after its own kind. All the future generations of these plants would be made according to the same pattern as the previous generations. And yet every plant is unique in the particular way it grows. Although we cannot prove there have never been two plants exactly alike, it certainly appears that way. Consider a whole field of wheat or corn, or the multitude of grass shoots growing in your lawn. For each and every one to be fashioned in a slightly different way is surely a marvelous thing. Only a very wise and powerful God could do something like that.

If we take time to look closely at these plants and compare them, we can see the wide variety within every kind of plant, such as in the many varieties of apples or corn. Sometimes these differences are only noticeable when the fruit appears. God has made this variety possible within the different kinds of plants, and He has allowed men to discover ways to develop new varieties. Sometimes a plant will produce a "sport," which is the name for a mutation that starts developing a different variety on some part of the plant. If the sport is a good one, it may be grafted into an existing plant to produce a new variety. Grafting has been done ever since Bible times to cultivate certain varieties. Men can also produce hybrids by cross-pollinating different varieties of the plant.

But all these varieties are within the limits set by God. It is not possible for one kind to evolve into another kind of plant, such as apples to oranges. We can identify and name all different kinds of plants because each reproduces after its kind. Radishes come from radish seeds, apples come from apple trees, pine cones from pine trees. This rule is true everywhere we look in the plant world. God ordained it that way, and the laws that God set in order at creation are still in effect today.

This was all arranged on the third day of creation. When God said the word, the world was immediately alive with beautiful vegetation. God was preparing the earth with an ample food supply for the animals and people He would create. So when Adam and Eve were formed several days later, don't you think they ate their veggies?

God saw that it was good. 13And the evening and the morning were the third day.

The Fourth Day: God Fills the Firmament

> ¹⁴*And God said, Let there be lights in the firmament of the heaven to divide the day from the night; and let them be for signs, and for seasons, and for days, and years:* ¹⁵*And let them be for lights in the firmament of the heaven to give light upon the earth: and it was so.* ¹⁶*And God made two great lights; the greater light to rule the day, and the lesser light to rule the night: he made the stars also.* ¹⁷*And God set them in the firmament of the heaven to give light upon the earth,* ¹⁸*And to rule over the day and over the night, and to divide the light from the darkness: and God saw that it was good.* ¹⁹*And the evening and the morning were the fourth day.*

As you will remember, nighttime and daytime had been happening since the very first day, but there was no sun, moon, or stars. Can you imagine what our world would be like without them? God provided for them on the fourth day of creation. He placed them in the firmament which He had prepared on the second day.

The sun was designed to rule the day. When we see where it is in the sky, we can get an idea of how much time is left in the day, or in which direction we are headed. The sun also affects the seasons as it moves north and south on its annual journey. It controls the length of daylight with shorter days in winter and longer days in summer. In the northern hemisphere the longest day is in June, while south of the equator the seasons are just the opposite, with winter in June and summer in December. As we pass from winter to summer, and the amount of daylight increases, the sun gradually warms the earth, causing seeds to germinate and spring from the soil. And as we continue toward winter once again, the daylight decreases, and the warmth leaves the ground and air. Some plants die each year when the cold comes, and others go dormant during the shorter days. The amount of light and heat affects many animals as well. When the cold weather limits the food supply, bears, squirrels, bees, and many other creatures survive from the extra they stored in the summertime, when food was abundant. All these changing patterns of life are caused by the changing position of the sun. God set it in the firmament on just the right course to make our earth suitable for all the living things that He would create.

The moon travels around the earth a little slower than the sun. Because its light is only a reflection of the sun's light, it is not as bright, and it changes according to how much of the sunlit side we can see. These changes are called the phases of the moon. Men have discovered that the ocean tides correspond with the position of the moon and its phases, and so the timing of tides can be predicted very precisely. And because the moon rules the night with its changing light, it affects the activities of many nocturnal creatures.

What would the sky be like at night without stars? Although there are stars in every direction, some shine brighter than others. People have given names to groups of bright stars, which are called constellations. In the northern hemisphere, the stars rotate around the North Star, which stays in the same place. Since the same stars can be seen from many places on earth, people have used them for thousands of years to travel in unfamiliar places, especially on the sea, where no landmarks can be seen. In the Bible we read about the wise men who saw a very special star that told them Christ the King had been born. They came a long way from the east to worship Him.

Read again from Psalm 19:

> ¹*The heavens declare the glory of God; and the firmament sheweth his handywork.* ²*Day unto day uttereth speech, and night unto night sheweth knowledge.* ³*There is no speech nor language, where their voice is not heard.*

People everywhere in the world have the witness of the starry heavens which testify of our marvelous Creator. No one has an excuse to say that God has not revealed Himself. Truly the heavens declare His glory.

Special Creation

We are surrounded by so many living things that it all seems quite normal to us and we usually don't think much about it. We only tend to notice when something goes wrong. Maybe the pea seeds we planted don't sprout, or maybe we get sick with the flu, or maybe a hurricane floods our whole city. But most of the time we are able to enjoy life without those problems. This is all because God made our world a very special place that is unlike anywhere else men have explored.

The Earth Is a Special Creation

There is only one earth, and it is God's centerpiece of creation. He planned it to be a home for all the living creatures He would make, and especially for people, the most important part of His creation. God enjoys everything He made, but He is most interested in us, because He made us to be able to communicate with Him, so He took great care in creating our home.

God placed the earth just where He wanted it to be. Then around it He wrapped the firmament, in which He placed the sun, moon, and stars—the *"host of heaven."* As they circle around us in their courses, they accomplish God's purpose in creating our calendar of signs and seasons, days and years.

When we study our world, we learn about the various climates where different kinds of plants and animals live. Many of these are teeming with all types of creatures that need just that sort of habitat to survive. Some plants only grow where there is a lot of rain, and others only in a desert. Some animals only live where it is very hot, and others only where it's cold. Yaks live high in the Himalayan mountains, and the astonishing humpback anglerfish lives deep down in the sea. Just about every place that people have looked on earth, they have found something God designed to live there. God designed us to live on land. And although most of the billions of people in the world live where it is not extremely dry, and where the temperature doesn't get very cold, God made us clever enough to learn how to live in almost any climate.

When you stop and think about it, we need several things in order to survive, such as air, food, and water. God has provided everything we need, with just the right amount of each. The marvelous water cycle brings rain, providing fresh water for us, as well as for the plants and animals. We are able to eat many kinds of food, which gives us energy. And the oxygen our bodies need all the time is taken from the air we breathe. Just like with building a house, God has made available all the materials that we need, and He designed our bodies like a well-working building crew that takes all those materials and puts them in just the right places to build our bodies and keep us alive and healthy. Just think how much God loves us, to create us so that we would enjoy eating! Even if our taste buds have been spoiled by sweets, we are still able to change and learn to like asparagus, spinach, peas, and other wholesome foods that give us strength. *"I will praise thee; for I am fearfully and wonderfully made: marvellous are thy works; and that my soul knoweth right well"* (Psalm 139:14).

Scientists have studied the stars, and sent rockets to explore the moon and planets. They have found these places to be very different from earth. The moon has no air to breathe, and the landscape is barren gray hills and valleys. The planet Venus is almost as large as the earth, but its atmosphere is dense and toxic to any life. It is also boiling hot, since it is much closer to the sun. The planet Mars on the other hand is much farther from the sun, so it is usually very cold. Most of the water is frozen solid, and the rest evaporates because the atmosphere is so light. Dust storms frequently swirl across the surface. The planets farther away have even more extreme conditions. They are all very interesting to study, and God enjoyed making them all different, but no one has found any other place good for life. There doesn't need to be, because God made the earth specially for us to live here.

Unbelievers imagine the earth as a planet spinning aimlessly through space. But it is a one-and-only special creation of God, the center of His attention, the home of the human family. We know this because God wanted us to know it, and had it recorded for us in the Bible. The very first place for people was the beautiful garden which God planted for Adam and Eve. It was perfect in every way, with everything God wanted them to have. How they must have enjoyed living there, cultivating the garden as God had appointed, and spending time with their Creator. Imagine being there with them, marveling as you see new plants springing forth from the ground, fresh blossoms bursting into bloom, and a mother deer nuzzling her wobbly fawn as it takes its first steps.

But when Adam and Eve accepted the suggestion of Satan to eat the forbidden fruit, disobeying God's command, everything was spoiled. As a judgment on their sin, they were driven from the lovely garden of Eden and had to make their home on their own. The earth was cursed, and the problems of evil have continued with us ever since.

Yet God has never given up on us. He has a special interest in every living thing, but especially you and me. He notices when a sparrow falls to the ground, and He knows the number of hairs on your head! He cares very much about how each of us are doing. Because God loves us so much, He sent His Son Jesus to earth so that we could be saved from our sins.

The Sun Is a Special Creation

The sun is special because God created it to serve the earth by giving it light. The stars also produce light, and sometimes people call the sun a star, but God made the sun unique to the earth to provide just the right amount of light we need. As its bright light shines on the earth, the earth becomes warmer. If the sun shone on the same place all the time, it would get too hot to live there, and too cold everywhere else in the shadow of night. But because God has caused the sun to circle completely around the world each day, the earth gets the right balance of warming during the day, and cooling during the night so it stays suitable for life. Also, if the sun were closer, the water would boil away, or if it were farther, we would all freeze. God put it at just the right distance so it would work for our good in every detail.

What is light, and how does it work? People that study light tell us it travels in waves called radiation, or rays. If you throw a stone in water you will notice ripples, which are small waves. If you go to the ocean, especially on a stormy day, you will see very large waves. A wave has a high point and a low point. The distance between the high points is called the wavelength. Light is sort of like the waves of water. The tremendous heat of the sun sends out rays in many different wavelengths, called the electromagnetic spectrum, and each wavelength has unique properties.

God made our eyes with special sensors to be able to see some of these waves, so we call that visible light. The colors we see come from different wavelengths of light. Red has a longer wavelength, and violet has a shorter wavelength. All the color wavelengths blended together make white light. A special instrument called a prism can bend a beam of white sunlight and separate the wavelengths, showing us all the different colors it has. This is how we see God's beautiful rainbows. The tiny drops of water in the clouds bend the sunbeams in a certain direction, which separates the colors. You can make your own rainbow on a sunny day by standing with your back to the sun and spraying mist into the air.

Just think how dull our world would be if we did not see all the different colors around us. These colors come from the rays that are reflected from the sunlight shining on the object. All objects either absorb or reflect light rays. When white sunlight shines on the grass, it absorbs all the rays except the green ones, which bounce off and enter our eyes so we see it. The way God designed our eyes is truly amazing. So many different parts work together to help us see. He gave us three kinds of cells called cones that enable us to detect red, green, and blue light. When these are combined together, we can see the other colors as well. Studies indicate that we can distinguish millions of shades of color. Some people are color blind, which means they are not able to see certain colors. I had a friend who could not tell reds and greens apart. This is a common type of color blindness, especially among men and boys, and occurs when the cones are damaged so that red and green objects tend to appear sort of murky yellow instead.

There are also other light rays that we cannot see. The shorter wavelengths in the spectrum beyond violet are called ultraviolet. Some insects and birds can see these rays. These kinds of rays from the sun stimulate our bodies to produce Vitamin D, which strengthens our bones, but too much causes sunburns and skin cancer. These rays are often used to kill germs. Shorter waves than these are x-rays, which special cameras can use to view the bones in our body. But they can increase risk to cancer if not used carefully.

In the other direction, infrared rays have longer wavelengths than the red we see. Things that are not hot enough to produce visible light can produce infrared light. Some snakes can sense these rays coming from warm-blooded animals, which helps them find food. Also, infrared cameras are used to detect how much heat is leaking from a building. After infrared is microwaves. If you have one of these special ovens, then your food is being cooked by light rays. Longer yet are radio waves, used for many kinds of communication.

The sun emits all these kinds of light rays, but God has designed the atmosphere of the earth to protect us by blocking most of the harmful rays. Yet you should never stare at the sun, because the intense light, especially the ultraviolet rays, can damage your ability to see.

Another very important aspect of light is that plants use it to grow. A special process called photosynthesis enables them to absorb the sunlight and convert it to energy. This is the foundation of the food chain, since all animals either eat plants or eat other animals that eat plants.

Now you can start to see how God placed the sun at just the right distance from the earth to make it productive. Without the light of the sun, everything would die. And just as the sun is the life-giving source for all living things, so Jesus, the Son of God, is the source of life for all who desire to serve God.

The Moon Is a Special Creation

The daily journey of the sun around the earth takes 24 hours. The moon's journey takes 24 hours and 49 minutes. Since it travels across the sky at a slower speed, the sun passes it every 29 ½ days, which is called a lunar month (*luna* is the Latin word for the moon). When the moon is in the same part of the sky as the sun, the sunlight is all shining on the far side, so we cannot see it. This is called the new moon. On very rare occasions, the moon is directly in front of the sun,

The following list shows approximately how the Hebrew calendar relates to our calendar, so when you read your Bible you can see what time of the year the events took place. At first the months were mostly numbered, but when the Jews were exiled in Babylon, they began using names for each of the months.

Because the Hebrew calendar is based on the lunar month of 29 or 30 days, there are about 11 extra days in a solar year. To keep the calendar from continually shifting seasons, in some years an extra "leap" month is added before the 12th month.

1	Nisan/Abib	March–April
2	Iyar/Zif	April–May
3	Sivan	May–June
4	Tammuz	June–July
5	Av	July–August
6	Elul	August–September
7	Tishri/Ethanim	September–October
8	Cheshvan/Bul	October–November
9	Kislev	November–December
10	Tevet	December–January
11	Shevat	January–February
12	Adar	February–March

causing the sunlight to disappear for a few minutes in the daytime. This is called a solar eclipse (*sol* is the Latin word for the sun). Half a month later, the moon is on the opposite side of the earth from the sun, and we see a full moon reflecting the sunlight at night. During a lunar eclipse, the earth's shadow passes across the full moon, turning it dark red.

The cycles of the sun and moon are very regular, and so even though it takes a lot of math calculations, the phases of the moon can be known ahead of time. These are often shown in calendars and almanacs. Abraham Lincoln was a lawyer before he was president of the

United States. In one court case, a witness testified that he saw something on a certain night by the bright light of the moon. But Lincoln showed by the almanac that there was no moonlight at the time, which proved that the person was lying.

The gravity of the moon pulls on the earth, which together with the gravity of the sun causes the ocean tides. Thus the timing of tides can be accurately predicted. Estimates of the expected tide height can be made, based on factors such as the shape of the ocean floor and coastline, as well as the latitude in relation to the moon, although the actual height of a particular tide is often affected by the weather. Farmers of many different times and cultures have believed that the phases of the moon affect the weather, particularly rainfall. Some of these beliefs seem to be based on superstitions, and careful studies have not been able to find any reliable connection.

The Stars Are a Separate Creation
"He made the stars also." When the sun sets, and the brightness of its light fades from the sky, we begin to see specks of light sprinkled through the heavens. The stars make light like our sun, but they are so much farther away that they are normally only seen at night. Some are brighter and closer than others. If you patiently counted all the stars you could see, you would find over 9000. With telescopes you can see many more that are fainter and farther away. In fact, there are so many that scientists cannot count each one. They can only count the number of stars in a small part of the sky, and then estimate how many there may be in the rest of the heavens—billions upon billions of stars. It is hard to comprehend numbers that are so big. And still they have not found them all. But God knows. The Bible says, *"He telleth the number of the stars; he calleth them all by their*

names" (Psalm 147:4). That should not surprise us, because He made each one.

People have given names to the groups of bright stars we can see, imagining them sort of like dot-to-dot pictures in the sky. These are called constellations, and the Bible mentions a few, such as in Job 38:31-32. Orion, which is commonly fancied to be a hunter, is visible from any part of the world, best seen just after nightfall January through March. The Big Dipper is also well-known in the Northern Hemisphere, and you can use it to find the North Star. Because this star stays in the same place while the others rotate around it, it can be used to tell direction at night. Before the end of slavery in the United States, many slaves escaped to freedom in Canada by following the North Star.

Sailors often used the stars to navigate as they traveled far from their familiar lands. A special instrument called a sextant was developed, which helped them know where they were by checking the position of the sun or stars.

If you are interested in studying more about the stars, a good place to start would be to get a star map. These special maps will help you locate many of the stars and constellations you can see during the changing seasons of the year. (Star maps and guides are available from Rod and Staff Publishers.)

Just imagine Adam and Eve before they went to bed their very first night. While the darkness deepened, they may well have looked up in wonder as the tiny points of light appeared. All the host of the starry heavens were there, declaring the glory of God. People have supposed that there may be other worlds like our own near some star far out in the firmament. But for all the many years they have searched, they have not been able to find any sign of life out in space. Life is a miracle, a special gift which God has given to us here on earth.

The Fifth Day: Marine and Avian Life

> [20]And God said, Let the waters bring forth abundantly the moving creature that hath life, and fowl that may fly above the earth in the open firmament of heaven. [21]And God created great whales, and every living creature that moveth, which the waters brought forth abundantly, after their kind, and every winged fowl after his kind: and God saw that it was good. [22]And God blessed them, saying, Be fruitful, and multiply, and fill the waters in the seas, and let fowl multiply in the earth. [23]And the evening and the morning were the fifth day.

God is the creator of life. Life cannot come from any other source. God had first created the seas and the sky without life, but on the fifth day He filled them with living creatures of every kind. Each of these living things, from the very smallest to the very largest, continues to reproduce after its kind.

Over two-thirds of the earth's surface is covered with water, which is filled with many kinds of marine animals in both the salt-water oceans and the fresh-water lakes and streams. The smallest known fish are the Paedocypris, which live in peat swamps in Southeast Asia, and only grow up to a centimeter long. The waters are also home to the largest animal in the world: the blue whale. This mammal can grow over 100 feet long— longer than two school buses—and weigh almost 200 tons. Then there are oysters and octopuses, crabs, clams, and crocodiles, catfish and frogfish, dolphins and dugongs, sponges and sea horses, eels, seals, and tuna, on and on and on and on. Don't you think that God likes variety?

If you have the opportunity, I encourage you to visit an aquarium where you can watch a large variety of fish and other ocean creatures. If you cannot do that, maybe you could go to a pet store that features fish. They often have many fresh-water fish, and sometimes even a few salt-water kinds. Some families purchase an aquarium of their own to enjoy watching and feeding small fish.

Avian refers to birds, which are fascinating creatures too. Some are very beautiful and some are hard to spot; some fly around the world and some don't fly at all. The smallest bird is the bee hummingbird of Cuba, which measures hardly more than 2 inches long (half of that is beak and tail) and is lighter than a penny. While it hovers to sip nectar, flapping its wings 50-80 times a second, its heart rate is over 1200 beats a minute! Contrast that with the largest living bird, the ostrich, which is found in certain parts of Africa. Some males reach 9 feet tall, and weigh up to 350 lbs. It is the only bird with two toes, and can run up to 40 mph. An ostrich egg omelet would be enough to feed a large family, because it weighs over 3 lbs, as much as two dozen chicken eggs.

Most birds (as well as mammals) are warm-blooded, which means their bodies try to keep a consistent temperature, no matter how hot or cold it is outside. Their bodies make heat by digesting food, which means they need to eat a lot, but it also means they can live even where it is very cold. Animals like fish and reptiles are called cold-blooded, because their body temperature changes with their environment. The temperature affects how active they are, but the advantage of slowing down in cold weather also means they don't have to eat much to stay alive during the winter. It's not easy to observe these changes in fish, because water tends to change temperature very slowly. But if you ever find a snake on a cold morning, it is very sluggish. By resting in the sunshine, it can warm up, and may be able to slither around quite well when it gets warm enough.

Our Creator God is a lover of life, color, and variety. We could never live long enough to learn all the marvels of creation. What seems an almost endless variety of living things testifies to the wisdom and power of our Creator. He has created all these things so they can live together on our earth along with the billions of people He made. *"And God saw that it was good."*

The Sixth Day: Land Animals and Man

²⁴And God said, Let the earth bring forth the living creature after his kind, cattle, and creeping thing, and beast of the earth after his kind: and it was so. ²⁵And God made the beast of the earth after his kind, and cattle after their kind, and every thing that creepeth upon the earth after his kind: and God saw that it was good.

As simple as that, God spoke, and animals appeared all over the land. Again we see great variety. God must have enjoyed making all sorts of creatures that are so different from us. What would you do if you had the neck of a giraffe, or the nose of an elephant? Your mother would despair finding shoes for you if you had hundreds of legs like a millipede. And you can be glad you don't have the spines of a porcupine, or the teeth of a warthog! But when scientists study even the strangest-looking animals, they find that God made each of them with a purpose.

Many animals are domesticated, which means that people take care of them as pets or livestock because they are very useful to us. The Bible calls them cattle, though in America we only use that word for cows. Here we get milk from cows and goats, wool from sheep, and eggs from chickens. Many different kinds of animals provide meat to eat, while horses and other strong animals have been used for work and travel. Because God made different animals to thrive in different climates, children in other countries are familiar with livestock you may have never seen. Llamas and alpacas are used in the Andes Mountains of South America, water buffalo in South Asia, and reindeer near the North Pole. God's imagination is infinitely greater than ours, and He made all these things possible for our needs and enjoyment. If you go to a zoo, you can see a few of the many, many different kinds of animals that God created.

As you read these two verses in Genesis, did you notice how many times it said, *"after his kind"*? Even after thousands of years every living creature continues to reproduce after its kind, because God designed it that way. Dogs have puppies, cats have kittens, and hens have chicks. One kind of animal doesn't give birth to another kind of animal. Yet within every kind no one has ever found two exactly alike. Even identical twins are different, or how would you ever tell them apart? Of course, one might look the same as another until you get to know them better and learn what makes each one unique. God in His wisdom provided these distinctions for us.

> ²⁶*And God said, Let us make man in our image, after our likeness: and let them have dominion over the fish of the sea, and over the fowl of the air, and over the cattle, and over all the earth, and over every creeping thing that creepeth upon the earth.* ²⁷*So God created man in his own image, in the image of God created he him; male and female created he them.* ²⁸*And God blessed them, and God said unto them, Be fruitful, and multiply, and replenish the earth, and subdue it: and have dominion over the fish of the sea, and over the fowl of the air, and over every living thing that moveth upon the earth.*

God made us special. We are the only ones made like Him. Physically, people are much like animals: we have a brain, a heart, blood, muscles, bones, etc. But God is not a physical being like that. God is a spirit who is intelligent, with the ability to think, choose, plan, create, and love. He also has great power and dominion, and has imparted to mankind dominion over all the other living creatures He has made. God created people with the ability to communicate with Him as well as one another. God made us intelligent, so we are able to choose and obey His instructions; able to take responsibility and carry out His plans. God made mankind in His own likeness by giving us many of His own abilities, but in a limited way because we live in human bodies. God gave us these abilities because He wanted people to have families and fill the earth and subdue it. And, as we will learn more in Genesis 2, so we could care for it and one another. This is what God's creation is all about—making a home for people who would choose to love and have fellowship with their Creator.

> ²⁹*And God said, Behold, I have given you every herb bearing seed, which is upon the face of all the earth, and every tree, in the which is the fruit of a tree yielding seed; to you it shall be for meat.* ³⁰*And to every beast of the earth, and to every fowl of the air, and to every thing that creepeth upon the earth, wherein there is life, I have given every green herb for meat: and it was so.*

When you start to study the amazing variety of animals that God created, you'll soon learn that they all have different eating habits. Now remember that God had already created the plants on the third day, so not only was there plenty of food to eat, but every animal had just the kind of food it needed. There was bamboo for pandas, wood for termites, flower blossoms full of nectar for bees and butterflies, nuts and seeds for squirrels, and of course plenty of grass for cows, horses, and sheep.

There was also a wide variety of fruits and vegetables for people to enjoy.

Since God provided plants for food, this indicates that none of the animals ate meat in the beginning. And so men and animals lived together without fear, since they weren't hunting one another. Adam could have petted a big lion and the lion would have simply wagged his tail. There would have been no need for sheep to be afraid of wolves, or mice to be afraid of cats—all ate vegetation.

So why do we, as well as many animals, eat meat now? After the Flood many things changed. Genesis 9:1-6 explains how God added animal meat to man's diet, and put the fear of man upon the animals.

Thank you, God, for telling us these many things about our world.

> [31]*And God saw every thing that he had made, and, behold, it was very good. And the evening and the morning were the sixth day.*

The Seventh Day: Rest

> ¹*Thus the heavens and the earth were finished, and all the host of them.* ²*And on the seventh day God ended his work which he had made; and he rested on the seventh day from all his work which he had made.* ³*And God blessed the seventh day, and sanctified it: because that in it he had rested from all his work which God created and made.*

Here we are at the end of the very first week. God could have made everything in a single day, or even in the blink of an eye, but He chose to do it in six days. And by resting on the seventh day, God set an example for work and rest every week as an example for us to follow. *"God blessed the seventh day, and sanctified it."* Something that is sanctified is set apart from anything unclean for special service to God.

The word *sabbath*, which refers to this special day of rest at the end of the week, was first mentioned when God brought the children of Israel out of Egypt. Because they were traveling through a desert where there was no food, God provided manna. This was small, seed-like thing which lay on the ground in the morning, and the people could go out and gather it to make bread. It would only last for a day before spoiling. But God gave special instructions: *"See, for that the Lord hath given you the sabbath, therefore he giveth you on the sixth day the bread of two days; abide ye every man in his place, let no man go out of his place on the seventh day"* (Exodus 16:29). The Lord Himself observed the sabbath: there was no manna available on the seventh day.

When God made His covenant with the children of Israel, He gave Moses the Ten Commandments, which included this one:

37

⁸Remember the sabbath day, to keep it holy. ⁹Six days shalt thou labour, and do all thy work: ¹⁰But the seventh day is the sabbath of the Lord thy God: in it thou shalt not do any work, thou, nor thy son, nor thy daughter, thy manservant, nor thy maidservant, nor thy cattle, nor thy stranger that is within thy gates: ¹¹For in six days the Lord made heaven and earth, the sea, and all that in them is, and rested the seventh day: wherefore the Lord blessed the sabbath day, and hallowed it.
(Exodus 20)

When Jesus died and rose again He fulfilled the Law of Moses. *"For Christ is the end of the law for righteousness to every one that believeth"* (Romans 10:4). The New Testament is a new covenant. *"In that he saith, A new covenant, he hath made the first old. Now that which decayeth and waxeth old is ready to vanish away"* (Hebrews 8:13). New Testament Christians do not live under the Ten Commandments that were given to the nation of Israel, but by the law of life in Christ Jesus. *"For the law of the Spirit of life in Christ Jesus hath made me free from the law of sin and death"* (Romans 8:2). *"The law of the Spirit of life"* controls the heart of the believer and results in godly living.

Jesus invites people to come to Him with their burden of sin in repentance, and find rest for their souls:

²⁸Come unto me, all ye that labour and are heavy laden, and I will give you rest. ²⁹Take my yoke upon you, and learn of me; for I am meek and lowly in heart: and ye shall find rest unto your souls. ³⁰For my yoke is easy, and my burden is light. (Matthew 11)

Jesus and His disciples often went to the synagogues on the sabbath, but seventh-day keeping was not included as part the gospel message they preached. The Christians gathered for worship together frequently (Acts 2:46-47). And they often met on the first day of the week, the day Jesus rose from the dead.

To observe a day of rest and worship each week is right and appropriate, but more importantly we need to be at rest in our heart and conscience. In the New Covenant, God wants us to be sanctified inside, set apart from our selfish ways to serve Him (Hebrews 4:10; Romans 12:1). This is true rest, and Jesus wants to give it to each of us. *"For thou, Lord, art good, and ready to forgive; and plenteous in mercy unto all them that call upon thee"* (Psalm 86:5). *"We which have believed do enter into rest"* (Hebrews 4:3).

Miracles: God Is Lord of Creation

When God created the heavens and the earth, He also created the forces that cause everything to work together. We cannot see these forces, but we can see the effects they have on everything God created. For example, when you jump up, the force of gravity brings you back down. If you are lost in the woods, a compass needle drawn by the force of the Earth's magnetic pole can help orient you in the right direction to bring you back home.

People call these forces the "the laws of nature," because God made them so consistent and orderly, and everything obeys them. God has not explained these forces in the Bible, but He has allowed men to discover many things about them. Scientists study these forces and try to describe how they work. These descriptions are used to predict what will happen in all sorts of situations in nature. Builders learn about these laws so their buildings won't fall down. Inventors learn about these laws so they can make better inventions. You can heat your home, fly in an airplane, or call your grandma on the other side of the country because many people have studied these laws, and then applied what they learned to make something useful. As scientists study and learn more, they sometimes have to make changes to their theories to match what actually happens. The forces themselves don't change, because they obey God, and He created them to work that way. Everything keeps happening just like He said for it to be, and will continue until He says otherwise. God is a God of order and purpose.

Since God is the one who made nature and its laws in the first place, He can make special events in nature for His purposes. When something happens that we can't explain by science, we call it a miracle. In such a case,

God may have used some part of His natural laws that we don't understand—or He may have simply used the creative power of His spoken word, just like He did when He made everything in the first place.

God uses miracles to get people's attention and show that He is God. We know He wants people who will choose to obey Him and be His people. The Bible tells us that *"the eyes of the Lord run to and fro throughout the whole earth, to shew himself strong in the behalf of them whose heart is perfect toward him"* (2 Chronicles 16:9). As we read the record of history, we find many places where God performed miracles to deliver His people, and also to bring judgment on those who disobey.

After Adam and Eve were cast out of Eden, their descendents turned away from God more and more. Men became exceedingly wicked, and their thoughts were only evil continually. It was so bad that the only righteous people left were Noah and his family. In this state of affairs, God stepped in and broke up all the fountains of the great deep and opened the windows of heaven, until the earth was covered with a flood of water. All living things on earth were destroyed, along with all the wicked people. But God saved Noah and his family and the animals that were with him in the ark because he obeyed.

At the time when Abraham was living in the land of Canaan, the nearby cities of Sodom and Gomorrah were full of exceedingly sinful people. God decided to destroy those cities as a judgment on their wickedness. But first He sent two angels to warn Abraham's nephew Lot, who was living in Sodom. After Lot left, God rained fire and brimstone and burned up the wicked cities.

When the Israelites were slaves in Egypt, God had a plan to deliver them to be His special chosen nation. He sent Moses to tell Pharaoh, the king of Egypt, to let the slaves go. When Pharaoh refused, God sent ten plagues that just about ruined the country, until finally Pharaoh himself demanded the Israelites to get out as fast as they could. But soon after they left, he changed his mind again and chased after them with his army until the Israelites were trapped between the army and the sea. Then God performed another miracle by making a special strong wind separate the waters so the Israelites could cross through the sea on dry ground. After they all got safely to the other side, the Egyptians tried to follow. But before the army could get across, God stopped holding the waters back, so the sea rushed back and drowned the Egyptian army. So God used the same miracle to save His people and also destroy their enemies.

Many miracles occurred during the 40 years the Israelites camped in the wilderness. In fact, the manna which they ate during that whole time was a daily miracle, a reminder that God was taking care of them. Then, when they were finally ready to enter Canaan, they found themselves at the Jordan River in flood season, when it overflowed its banks. Once again God miraculously held up the waters, making a way for His people to cross over on dry ground into their new homeland.

God knew there were many enemies the Israelites would have to conquer in this land. As long as they trusted in God, He caused miracles to happen to help them win. When they came to attack Jericho, God caused the wall to fall down and the people to be destroyed, except for Rahab and her family, who wanted to join God's people. Later, in a great battle against the evil Amorites, God helped by casting huge hailstones upon them, and even causing the sun and moon to stand still for a whole day, until Joshua and the Israelites had defeated the enemy.

The Bible tells us about many other amazing things God has done to help His people and bring judgment on the wicked. Sometimes He uses natural events, such as drought or storms, or needed rain. We call these things God's Providence, because He is caring and providing for His people. Sometimes He does things that are supernatural, things that science theories can't explain, like when He made the whole Syrian army blind for a while in answer to Elisha's prayer (2 Kings 6:18), or when He saved Shadrach, Meshach, and Abednego from any hurt when they were cast into a blazing furnace (Daniel 3). These things remind us that God is greater than anything He made, and that He can use His power whenever He wants to change something.

No matter what happens in life, God is in control. He may allow times of suffering, even for His own people, but He always has good plans in mind, and He knows what is truly best for us (Jeremiah 29:11). We may not always understand, but if we love God, and simply trust and obey Him, we never need to be afraid. He puts peace in the hearts of His children, for we know He will take care of us, whether in life or in death.

God made everything by simply speaking the word, and it was so. The world continues, we live and breathe, and days go by, all because His word keeps things going. And the Bible also tells us there will come a day when God will speak the word, and the heaven and the earth and time and all the "laws of nature" will come to an end. That is when the final judgment will be, when all the wicked and disobedient people will be sent away from God and cast into hell. It is also the time when God will come to gather all those who love Him, and they will get to go live with Him forever and ever in the glorious home He has prepared ever since the very beginning. A home where there is no evil, no temptations, and no suffering.

No one but God knows when that time will be, but we can be sure it will be the best time. Let us love and serve Him now, so we'll be ready at any time.

Made in the Image of God

As we learned when studying the Creation Week recorded in Genesis 1, man was created on the sixth day.

> ²⁶*And God said, Let us make man in our image, after our likeness: and let them have dominion over the fish of the sea, and over the fowl of the air, and over the cattle, and over all the earth, and over every creeping thing that creepeth upon the earth.* ²⁷*So God created man in his own image, in the image of God created he him; male and female created he them.*

The second chapter of Genesis gives us some additional details of how He went about it:

> ⁷*And the Lord God formed man of the dust of the ground, and breathed into his nostrils the breath of life; and man became a living soul.*

God was doing something very special. He had already made everything else, and now He was ready to make His final creation. When we create something new with our hands, we concentrate with our eyes sharply focused on what we are doing. Here we find that God took some of the dust of the ground, and with it He fashioned a single object. This masterpiece of creation would be called Adam—the Hebrew word for *man*—who was made "*in the image of God.*"

An image is a resemblance, like a statue or picture of someone, which is made to resemble that person, showing what he is like. Remember, being made like God does not mean that God has a physical body like ours, but that we have abilities like Him which none of the animals have.

We can learn what it means to be like God by studying animals to see how we are different from them, and by studying the Bible to see how we are made like God.

The first verse in the Bible tells us that God creates—and we've been learning about His creative work all along. God has given man the ability to create as well. We certainly can't make something out of nothing by simply speaking the word, like God can. But we can think and imagine, consider different ideas, choose how to make what we have in mind, and find or invent tools that help make life easier. Animals are guided by instinct, which is just how God designed them to automatically respond, rather than really studying and learning new ways of doing things. Only people can change the kind of house they want to have, choose the food they want to eat, or the games they wish to play. God gave people the opportunity to make many choices that the animals do not have.

People also have God's ability to enjoy beauty. God looked at what He had made and saw that it was good. He made spectacular sunsets, beautiful birds, and detailed designs. How many animals do you know that enjoy sight-seeing or listening to birdsong by a sparkling stream? People not only appreciate the beautiful things God made, but use their own creative abilities to make life more enjoyable. We find pleasure in poetry, delight in designing our homes, enjoy beautiful music, and take more photos than you can imagine.

Another difference we see is that God gave man dominion over all the other creatures. Dominion means having power and control. You and I were born as tiny, helpless babies that needed to be fed and protected and taught. Yet we all have potential for dominion. As we grow, we gain understanding and increase in wisdom by experience and learning day by day. But Adam wasn't born as a baby. Even though he was brand new in the world, God had made him already a mature person, with all the wisdom and knowledge he needed to have dominion.

Dominion is both a privilege and a responsibility, and one of the first jobs God gave Adam was to name the animals. God *"brought them unto Adam to see what he would call them: and whatsoever Adam called every living creature, that was the name thereof"* (Genesis 2:19). When your parents named you, they probably thought about how the name sounds, or people they admired who had that name, or what the name means, and perhaps they waited until you were born to see what you looked like as well. God had given Adam the intelligence to be able to study all the many different animals God showed him, and decide on a good name for each one right away. Adam was probably the most intelligent man who ever lived, because God had made him just right, and his mind was not affected by the corruption which is caused by sin.

God could have made both a man and a woman out of the dust of the ground, but He didn't. He did something far more wonderful. Of all the animals that Adam named there was not one suitable for him as a companion. So God provided a wife for him in a marvelous way. Here is what the Bible tells us:

> [21]*And the Lord God caused a deep sleep to fall upon Adam, and he slept: and he took one of his ribs, and closed up the flesh instead thereof;* [22]*And the rib, which the Lord God had taken from man, made he a woman, and brought her unto the man.* [23]*And Adam said, This is now bone of my bones, and flesh of my flesh: she shall be called Woman, because she was taken out of Man.* [24]*Therefore shall a man leave his father and his mother, and shall cleave unto his wife: and they shall be one flesh.*

Amazing! Adam had been formed from the dust, but rather than starting again from scratch, God made the woman from the man. She was fashioned from Adam's rib, something close to his heart, showing that God intended them to have such a close connection that they would be counted as one. That connection is called marriage. This is the foundation of the home and family, God's plan for people to be born and nurtured and taught how to live. A husband and wife have a very special and solemn responsibility to help each other, and to raise the children God gives them. When some people asked Jesus if it was all right to break a marriage by getting divorced, Jesus told them:

> *4Have ye not read, that he which made them at the beginning made them male and female, 5And said, For this cause shall a man leave father and mother, and shall cleave to his wife: and they twain shall be one flesh? 6Wherefore they are no more twain, but one flesh. What therefore God hath joined together, let not man put asunder.* (Matthew 19)

God made marriage to last as long as the husband and wife are both living (Romans 7:2). The family unit is sacred in His sight.

Look back at Genesis 1:26 and notice that God spoke of Himself in the plural: "*Let us make man in our image, after our likeness.*" The fact that God is one and yet more than one is not easy to understand. He reveals Himself to us in three different roles: Father, Son, and Holy Spirit. We call this the Trinity, a word which means threefold. We have already read about the Spirit, when He moved upon the waters. And the New Testament tells us that the Son was present, for "*All things were made by him*" (John 1:3). Together with the Father they work in perfect harmony.

By making man male and female that would work together in marriage as one, God has given us a picture to help us understand how He works as one in the Godhead. Though each Person in the Godhead is equally God, yet the Father holds the authority, and the Son and Spirit cooperate fully in carrying out His plans. He designed the marriage union to reflect this relationship by giving the responsibility of authority to the husband, and role of submission to the wife, even though they are equal persons made by God. In addition to their unique roles, consider also how men and women each tend to have unique abilities and personality traits that complement each other. When both work together in harmony, a couple can begin to reflect the image of our Creator.

A very significant aspect of this is communication, the ability to share thoughts with someone else. Of course, animals communicate after a fashion, as they relate to their communities and other creatures. But people are able to share complex ideas and relate to one another so deeply because God Himself is a communicator. We have seen this throughout the Creation Week, for God did not simply think the world into existence, He spoke. The Godhead of Father, Son, and Spirit spoke among Themselves, and no doubt they spoke with the angels, who *"shouted for joy"* when God made the world (Job 38:7). Although we're made like God, we're still limited. I'm sure each of us is familiar with the frustration of being misunderstood by someone else. Yet even though our communication sometimes breaks down, we have still within us the possibility of understanding not only other people, but also God Himself, when He speaks to us through His Word and by His Spirit.

This brings us to the most important aspect of being made in the image of God. When God formed the first human body, He *"breathed into his nostrils the breath of life; and man became a living soul.*" You are a soul, and your soul is you. You and I live in a human body. The Bible describes the body as a house for the soul. But God is a spirit, and He has put within each of us a spirit as well, which is how He communicates with us. *"There is a spirit in man: and the inspiration of the Almighty giveth them understanding"* (Job 32:8). This spirit is inside the soul like the marrow inside the bone (Hebrews 4:12). The words spirit and soul are often used to describe the inner part of us that is not material. Doctors don't find it when they do surgery, and scientists can't see it when they study the brain, but we know it's there because God tells us in the Bible. And, like the wind, though we can't see it, we can see its effects.

Little children growing up do not realize that they are a soul, for they are just learning about living in a body. But everyone is born with a sin nature that does not like to obey, so children soon start to do many naughty things. Yet they are innocent and carefree, because they don't realize they are disobeying God. If their parents correct and train them according to the Bible, it will help develop the child's conscience. As a child begins to develop into adulthood, he discovers that he is no longer carefree, and his conscience tells him something is wrong. This "awakening" of the soul makes him aware that he is accountable to God for his conduct, and because of sin—disobedience to God—he is often afraid of death. The Spirit of God calls to his soul to repent and come to Him. If he ignores God's call, Satan deceives him and makes him believe that he is in control of his life. But in reality he is simply blind to what drives him to go deeper in sin, ignoring God. However, we can never completely escape God, for our souls are always aware of the One who created us.

So when we find our hearts are troubled, our consciences accusing us, it is because God wants us to repent and turn to Him. Because He loves us so much and doesn't want us to be separated from Him, He sent His own Son into the world to solve the problem. Jesus came to live a human life like us, and then to give His life as a sacrifice, dying in our place. By faith in Jesus we can be forgiven and have our souls cleansed from sin so that we can live lives acceptable to Him. There is no reason to live under condemnation when God provided so great a salvation!

Animals also have the breath of life. They react and experience emotions. They praise and glorify God by doing just what He planned for them to do when He made them. But animals don't have a soul that can communicate with God like we can. Nor do they keep living after their body dies like we do. When an animal dies, it simply returns to dust, but when our body dies, then *"the spirit shall return unto God who gave it"* (Ecclesiastes 12:7).

By giving us spirits, God made us moral beings, knowing right and wrong, which means we are responsible for choosing whether to obey or not. When we obey God, we commune with Him and worship Him through the spirit. This is called having spiritual life, because we are connected to God, who is the source of life. Jesus compared it to a branch that gets its life by being connected to a vine (John 15:1-8). Spiritual life is a precious gift that can never be treasured too highly. God made Adam the way He wanted us all to be. Just imagine being there as God puts the finishing touches on His final creation, and then gently breathes His life into man. Watch Adam open his eyes in this wonderful new world and gaze in adoration at God!

The Garden of Eden

*8And the Lord God planted a garden eastward
in Eden; and there he put the man whom he
had formed. 9And out of the ground made the
Lord God to grow every tree that is pleasant to
the sight, and good for food; the tree of life
also in the midst of the garden, and the tree of
knowledge of good and evil.... 15And the Lord
God took the man, and put him into the
garden of Eden to dress it and to keep it.*

God had made the whole world with people in mind,
but the first home He prepared was a special garden.
Here Adam and Eve began their lifework, for God had
given them the job of cultivating the garden. How these
first farmers must have enjoyed their work in this brand
new world! God had provided everything their hearts
could desire. They had each other and a free and open
relationship with God who came to visit with them. What
would they have talked about? Did God tell them how He
created the world, just as we have read in Genesis 1?
Would He have explained why He made the many
different plants and animals around them? The Bible
doesn't tell us those things, but they must have had
many an enjoyable time. They had everything they
needed to live happy, useful lives.

You probably noticed that God placed two special trees
in the middle of the garden. One was the tree of life and
one was the tree of the knowledge of good and evil. They
probably looked a lot like the other trees in the garden,
which were *"pleasant to the sight, and good for food."*

*16And the Lord God commanded the man,
saying, Of every tree of the garden thou
mayest freely eat: 17But of the tree of the*

knowledge of good and evil, thou shalt not eat of it: for in the day that thou eatest thereof thou shalt surely die.

God was not being mean by putting this forbidden tree in the garden. By making this rule, He was in fact giving mankind greater freedom than any other creature. The animals simply choose according to the way God made their minds to work, but God gave us the freedom of moral choice. This means we can know the difference between right and wrong, and choose whether or not to obey. God does not force us to obey Him. Also, God gave Adam fair warning about death. Adam would have understood that God was not talking about Adam's physical body, but about his living soul.

So Adam and Eve could live happily in the garden as long as they obeyed God and avoided the tree of the knowledge of good and evil. After all, they could eat the fruit of every other tree, including the wonderful tree of life. God had provided for all their needs, and even gave them an abundance of good options to enjoy. God's way is always the best way, and leads to a happy and fulfilling life.

What would it have been like to live and work in that beautiful garden? Many things were different back then. For one thing, it did not rain. *"But there went up a mist from the earth, and watered the whole face of the ground"* (Genesis 2:6), *"And a river went out of Eden to water the garden"* (verse 10). The Bible doesn't give any more details, so we don't know just how it all worked. Years later, when God brought judgment on the world in Noah's time because of sin, He caused it to rain for forty days. *"Whereby the world that then was, being overflowed with water, perished"* (2 Peter 3:6). If the garden was still existing then, the Flood would have destroyed it. Since that time, our world has been a much different place.

Even though we don't have a beautiful garden home to live in, like Adam and Eve, we can still find the fingerprints of God's creation all around us in His amazing world. And we still are faced with the same kind of choices that they had. We can choose a life of obedience to God, or we can choose to disobey. Either way has consequences, and what we choose will determine our destiny.

For those who serve the Lord, heaven is our garden of Eden—but even better. For one thing, unlike the first one, in that final home there will be no tree of the knowledge of good and evil. In this life we are being tested whether or not we will choose God and His way. His way really is the best way, for He knows the end result of every choice we can make. He has prepared a heavenly home filled with every good thing, and where nothing is forbidden. If we are faithful here, we may freely eat of the tree of life and drink of the pure river of life there. And best of all, we will forever be with the One who created us. God loves us greatly, and longs for us to be with Him.

The Serpent Deceives Eve

In a brand new world full of every good thing God had made, what could possibly go wrong? Adam and Eve had been carefully warned against eating from the tree of the knowledge of good and evil, and I'm sure they cheerfully obeyed. Like the children of a loving father, they trusted God to provide for all their needs. And He did. They had no reason to doubt Him.

But as we continue reading in the Bible, we will soon realize that God has an enemy who seeks to destroy all the good God does. This enemy is called Satan, "one who opposes." Because Adam and Eve were God's most special creation, Satan especially wanted to destroy their beautiful relationship with God. Just as God is full of every good thing, Satan is full of hate and harm. In the New Testament he is called the devil, which means someone who falsely accuses to cause harm. Jesus said, *"He was a murderer from the beginning, and abode not in the truth, because there is no truth in him. When he speaketh a lie, he speaketh of his own: for he is a liar, and the father of it"* (John 8:44).

The devil is very dangerous, but we don't need to be afraid of him as long as we obey God, for God is much more powerful, and is able to protect us from any harm. In fact, God is so powerful that Satan cannot even come near God's people unless He allows it. But now we will read how God allowed Satan to come into the garden of Eden as a test, to see whom Adam and Eve would choose to obey. Since Satan is very clever, he spoke to Eve through one of the animals God had made. And this is the record God gave us, to show us why there is so much sin and evil in the world today:

> ¹*Now the serpent was more subtil than any beast of the field which the Lord God had*

made. And he said unto the woman, Yea, hath God said, Ye shall not eat of every tree of the garden?

²And the woman said unto the serpent, We may eat of the fruit of the trees of the garden: ³But of the fruit of the tree which is in the midst of the garden, God hath said, Ye shall not eat of it, neither shall ye touch it, lest ye die.

⁴And the serpent said unto the woman, Ye shall not surely die: ⁵For God doth know that in the day ye eat thereof, then your eyes shall be opened, and ye shall be as gods, knowing good and evil.

⁶And when the woman saw that the tree was good for food, and that it was pleasant to the eyes, and a tree to be desired to make one wise, she took of the fruit thereof, and did eat, and gave also unto her husband with her; and he did eat.

Do you see how very cunningly the truth was twisted? Satan knows that an outright lie has no appeal to those who know the truth, so he takes the pure truth and mixes in the poison of a lie. His deception is made all the more effective by cleverly hiding the terrible results of wrongdoing from our eyes. He blinded Eve back then, and he still blinds people today.

In the garden of Eden Adam and Eve had a perfect situation. They had pleasant surroundings, plenty of delicious food, and sweet fellowship with their Creator. The only way Satan could deceive them was by making them dissatisfied in some way. It is not wrong for us to desire some good thing that we don't have, but dissatisfaction with one's blessings is often a first step to sin. So Satan planted a desire in Eve for something more than what she presently had—something she did not need, and that would actually cause her trouble. But she followed his suggestion without stopping to consider if everything he said was true. Much of the advertising done today uses these same methods. Beware! You cannot be tempted to buy a new gadget as long as you are satisfied with what you already have. Advertisements often try to create dissatisfaction by getting you to imagine how much better life would be if you had the product or service being offered. Sound familiar? Sometimes young people get dissatisfied with their home or parents. They think that the freedoms and blessings they already enjoy are not enough, and decide it must be better somewhere else.

But is that true? People become deceived when they believe something that is not true. God had told Adam the truth about the tree of the knowledge of good and evil. But the serpent painted a completely different picture to Eve. She listened as he placed deceptive questions in her mind. *"Yea, hath God said?"* The seed of doubt grew as he suggested that God was really withholding something good from her. When he said, *"Ye shall not surely die,"* it was but a half-truth, for he spoke only of her body, not of her soul. He held before her all the advantages of disobedience: this wonderful fruit would make her as wise as God. Satan made it all look so good, and the attractive tree looked innocent enough. The terrible results of disobedience were carefully hidden, and by now God's warning was probably forgotten in imagining what the promised benefits would be like. Satan always does that, blinding people to the outcome of sin. That is what got Eve in trouble, and it still gets people in trouble today. The Bible says, *"the wages of sin is death"* (Romans 6:23), yet many people think they will get by somehow. That is how deception works.

Eve, Eve, stop and think! Remember God's warning! The One who made you and loves you knows what is best for you! But with her thoughts full of Satan's promises, she acted. She reached out in disobedience, took the fruit, and ate it. And then Eve did what people often do when they sin. She convinced Adam to eat some, too. It is common for people who do wrong to want others to do the same. Watch out! Sometimes Satan works through others to tempt us to sin—and that person may even be our best friend!

The Bible tells us that Adam was not deceived as Eve was (1 Timothy 2:14). When Adam ate, he knew full well he was disobeying God. In a way this was even worse than Eve's sin. This is called presumptuous sin. The psalmist wrote, *"Keep back thy servant also from presumptuous sins; let them not have dominion over me: then shall I be upright, and I shall be innocent from the great transgression"* (Psalm 19:13). But whether we are deceived or sin willfully, being aware that we are doing wrong, the results are the same.

So did Adam and Eve die the same day that they ate the forbidden fruit?

Well, their bodies did not die that day, but something far worse happened, just like God said it would. Remember, their souls had been created alive to God, having sweet communion with Him and a clear conscience. Their sweet relationship with God died that day, and now their souls were dead souls. Separation from God is a more terrible death than physical death. As we will see later, Adam and Eve were driven from the garden and the tree of life, and in time their bodies also died. Thus they learned the truth. Satan was proved to be a liar, for they died as God had said.

Satan has not changed: he still makes good things look bad, and bad things look good. He still deceives people into thinking they can do wrong and get by with it somehow. Yet even if people seem to get by without consequence in this life, they still must face God and answer for what they have done.

What we have read in Genesis 3 is often referred to as the Fall of Man, for those two were the only ones in the world at the time. And fall they did from their beautiful relationship with their Creator. Sin still separates from God. But thanks be to God that through Jesus our relationship can be restored—we can be forgiven and delivered from disobedience to live once again with a clear conscience before our heavenly Father.

You Can't Do Wrong and Get By

Be not deceived; God is not mocked: for whatsoever a man soweth, that shall he also reap. Gal.6:7
For God shall bring every work into judgment... whether it be good, or whether it be evil. Ec.12:14

1. There's a God who's stand-ing   at heav-en's door, He's look-ing this
2. Out   in-to   the   dark-ness you a-lone may go, And seeds for the
3. Yes,   He knows your se-crets, eve-ry-thing you do, He knows that your

u - ni-verse o'er; And He sees each mor-tal   with a search-ing eye,
wicked one sow; There's an eye that's watching from the throne on high,
life is un-true; You can ne'er de-ceive Him, there's no use   to   try,

You can't do wrong and get by.   You can't do wrong and get by,

No mat-ter how much you may try;   Noth-ing hid-den can be,

eve-ry-thing He doth see, You can't do wrong and get   by.

WORDS and MUSIC: Lethal A. Ellis, 1929. Public Domain.

How Disobedience Affected Adam and Eve

Failure to believe and obey God brings serious results: sometimes right away, sometimes years later, and sometimes forever. As you read the following Scriptures you will see the serious results that Satan had hidden from Adam and Eve. The wonderful dream that Satan placed in their minds turned into a terrible mess. Here we see their troubles begin:

> *⁷And the eyes of them both were opened, and they knew that they were naked; and they sewed fig leaves together, and made themselves aprons.*

I doubt Adam and Eve were expecting that. Before they disobeyed God, they had been innocent in His sight, so they did not need clothing. But now that innocence was gone. There was evil in their hearts because of sin. Filled with shame, they immediately tried to find something to cover their bodies. Sewing together fig-leaf aprons was as far as they got in their first attempt at making clothes.

God knew that their meager covering was not good enough, and so *"Unto Adam also and to his wife did the Lord God make coats of skins, and clothed them"* (verse 21). Since we are sons and daughters of Adam, living in a sinful society and knowing good and evil, we also need to be fully clothed. God gives us instructions in the Bible on how He expects us to clothe ourselves, beginning with a pure and humble heart. Those who do not cover their bodies properly are walking in disobedience to God and are adding sin to sin.

In order for God to provide Adam and Eve with coats of skin, we presume it was necessary for animals to die and for blood to be shed. What were those animals? The

Bible does not say, but because sin offerings in the Old Testament were usually lambs, perhaps God took innocent lambs as the first sacrifice to set the example. We know that He already had a plan in mind to solve the problem of sin, and when Jesus came to be a sacrifice for us, He was announced as *"the Lamb of God, which taketh away the sin of the world"* (John 1:29).

But we are getting ahead in the record, so let us go back and find out what happened first after Adam and Eve had sewn their fig-leaf aprons:

> *⁸And they heard the voice of the Lord God walking in the garden in the cool of the day: and Adam and his wife hid themselves from the presence of the Lord God amongst the trees of the garden.*

Why did they run and hide? For the first time, Adam and Eve felt guilty, and they did not want God to see them. When we are doing what is right, we do not feel the need to hide because we have a clear conscience. Being guilty gives us an awful feeling. Adam and Eve discovered this when they disobeyed God, and it still happens when people sin today. Guilt causes children to hide from their parents and grownups to hide from the policeman. Jesus said, *"Men loved darkness rather than light, because their deeds were evil"* (John 3:19).

> *⁹And the Lord God called unto Adam, and said unto him, Where art thou?*
> *¹⁰And he said, I heard thy voice in the garden, and I was afraid, because I was naked; and I hid myself.*

Fear follows disobedience and sin. You see, God is pure and holy, and that is what causes fear in the sinner.

The only way to get rid of guilt and fear is to repent of our sin and find forgiveness in Christ. Some people carry guilt their whole lifetime. That is an awful way to live. Thank God, Jesus came so we can live without being afraid.

> [11]And [God] said, Who told thee that thou wast naked? Hast thou eaten of the tree, whereof I commanded thee that thou shouldest not eat?
> [12]And the man said, The woman whom thou gavest to be with me, she gave me of the tree, and I did eat.
> [13]And the Lord God said unto the woman, What is this that thou hast done? And the woman said, The serpent beguiled me, and I did eat.

So whose fault was it? When guilty people are caught, they often give excuses or try to blame others for what happened. Adam blamed God for giving him the wife that gave him the fruit. Then Eve blamed the serpent. Why do people blame their problems on others? Simply because they do not want to take responsibility for their own sin. It started right back there when Adam and Eve sinned and continues to this day. Did you ever blame someone else for what you did? You might hide your wrongs, but just remember, God knows all about it. In His great love for us, He wants to help us get right again, but the blame game only makes the problem bigger. Disobedience makes life miserable!

Do you think Adam and Eve expected all these troubles? Of course not! Hiding the truth about the consequences of sin is a big part of Satan's deception. Was he there to help them out when they were discovered? Not really! The only "help" Satan offers is to try to escape the consequences by running farther away from the right, and that only makes matters worse. Turning away from God and listening to Satan is the reason for all the wickedness in our world today.

Sowing and Reaping

There is a natural law of sowing and reaping. If we sow corn, we can expect to reap corn. If we sow ragweed, we can expect to reap ragweed. There is a similar law at work in each of our lives:

> *7Be not deceived; God is not mocked: for whatsoever a man soweth, that shall he also reap. 8For he that soweth to his flesh shall of the flesh reap corruption; but he that soweth to the Spirit shall of the Spirit reap life everlasting.* (Galatians 6)

God has given us the opportunity to make many choices in life. We can choose what is right or we can choose what is wrong—God gives us that privilege. But God does not give us the ability to control the outcome of our choices. Choices have consequences. Sometimes we reap right away and other times the reaping comes later. But don't be deceived, God controls the outcome. If we make bad choices, we can repent and be forgiven, but we still may need to reap the results of our sin in this life. When tempted to do wrong, do not forget the law of sowing and reaping. The full harvest will often be hidden from our eyes, but it is sure to come.

And so it was with Adam and Eve. The God who had so marvelously created and blessed them now became their judge. They had sown to satisfy their own desires (the flesh) and must now reap the results in their lives. Disobedience is sin, and it always requires punishment. Never forget that.

> *14And the Lord God said unto the serpent, Because thou hast done this, thou art cursed above all cattle, and above every beast of the*

field; upon thy belly shalt thou go, and dust shalt thou eat all the days of thy life. (Genesis 3)

It appears that at first the serpent may have had legs like most other land creatures. But because Satan had entered into this creature to tempt Eve, it was cursed to slither in the dust. This does not mean that God hates snakes, but it serves as a continual reminder that sin has serious consequences. Nor do we need to be afraid that snakes are evil, because Satan cannot enter any of God's creatures unless He allows it. If we are faithful in obeying God, He restricts what Satan can do in our lives. Verse 15 tells more of God's judgement on Satan, but we will study that in the next lesson.

16Unto the woman he said, I will greatly multiply thy sorrow and thy conception; in sorrow thou shalt bring forth children; and thy desire shall be to thy husband, and he shall rule over thee.

It was the woman who was deceived and who then gave to her husband to eat of the tree. Because she obeyed the voice of the Deceiver, two judgments of God came upon her. First, childbearing would not be easy for her, and second, she would be under the rule of her husband. These two judgments are still in effect today. Many women try to avoid them, but in so doing they suffer other consequences. They cannot escape reaping for resisting God's laws.

17And unto Adam he said, Because thou hast hearkened unto the voice of thy wife, and hast eaten of the tree, of which I commanded thee, saying, Thou shalt not eat of it: cursed is the ground for thy sake; in sorrow shalt thou eat of it all the days of thy life; ¹⁸*Thorns also and thistles shall it bring forth to thee; and thou shalt eat the herb of the field;* ¹⁹*In the sweat of thy face shalt thou eat bread, till thou return unto the ground; for out of it wast thou taken: for dust thou art, and unto dust shalt thou return.*

Did you ever wonder why there are thorns and thistles? Or why farming and gardening are hard work that make people sweat? Now you know. Because of sin, all the descendents of Adam have had to live with these consequences. Why all these punishments? It reminds us of our responsibility to God, and our need to come back to Him. For God told Adam that his body would eventually wear out and die. *"Then shall the dust return to the earth as it was: and the spirit shall return unto God who gave it"* (Ecclesiastes 12:7).

²²*And the Lord God said, Behold, the man is become as one of us, to know good and evil: and now, lest he put forth his hand, and take also of the tree of life, and eat, and live for ever:* ²³*Therefore the Lord God sent him forth from the garden of Eden, to till the ground from whence he was taken.* ²⁴*So he drove out the man; and he placed at the east of the garden of Eden Cherubims, and a flaming sword which turned every way, to keep the way of the tree of life.*

This judgment may seem unkind, but there was really much mercy in it, for God knows the future. He did not want Adam and Eve to have to live here forever. More than that, He knew it would be terrible for people with evil hearts to be continually spreading evil on earth without end. There is mercy in every judgment of God.

In His mercy, God does not always punish people for sin right away. He gives them opportunity to repent (2 Peter 3:9). But Satan uses God's mercy to deceive people. Because they often do not receive their full punishment immediately, Satan makes them believe that they will get by with sin. Consider this verse in the Bible: *"Because sentence against an evil work is not executed speedily, therefore the heart of the sons of men is fully set in them to do evil"* (Ecclesiastes 8:11). Don't get caught in that trap. Remember that God knows all about your sins, and sooner or later you will need to face them. So do it now! Read on.

The Love and Mercy of God

Was there no hope for Adam and Eve? Would they be separated from God forever? What about their children and all those that would follow after? Would they all be lost and suffer in hell forever?

Adam and Eve were no longer living souls, because they had lost their wonderful relationship with God. With that fellowship broken, their souls were dead. They had fallen from obedience, and must suffer the consequences. Things would never be the same. Their world was no longer a paradise because of the curse, and the children born into such a world would inherit their own fallen nature, having a natural impulse to disobey. *"Wherefore, as by one man sin entered into the world, and death by sin; and so death passed upon all men, for that all have sinned"* (Romans 5:12). Sinners are often said to be "lost," for they have lost the right way, and are destined to eternal separation from God.

When we have lost something we love and value, we want to find it again. If it is broken, we want to fix it. A good relationship with God is of great value. When Satan tempts us to disobey, he will try to make us forget that fact, but God never forgets. In spite of their disobedience, God still loved Adam and Eve. After all, they were the first members of the human race, the ones He had made in His own image. In fact, God values us so greatly that a single soul is worth more to Him than everything else He has made here. Can you imagine such love?

It should not surprise us then to learn that God had a plan to recover what was lost. A plan that would fix what was broken, and save mankind from the final consequence of sin: eternal death and separation from Himself forever. It was a plan so great that only the mind of God could create it, and only the power of God could accomplish it.

The first inkling we are given of such a plan is found in what God said to the serpent:

> *¹⁵And I will put enmity between thee and the woman, and between thy seed and her seed; it shall bruise thy head, and thou shalt bruise his heel.*

This judgment was actually a prophecy upon Satan, who was working through the serpent. God revealed that there would come a day when a descendant of *"the woman"*—Jesus Christ, who was also the son of God—would be victorious over Satan. Satan would cause Jesus to be crucified (bruise His heel), but Jesus would rise from the dead and bruise Satan's head. Satan's power would be broken, so people could be restored to a right relationship with God once again. Christ would bear the consequence for our sin, dying in our place, so we wouldn't have to die. By sacrificing His own Son, God would make it possible for anyone to have a part in this salvation when they come to Him in faith to be forgiven.

But as the guilty husband and wife received their judgment from God that day in the garden of Eden, they could not comprehend all this, for God would only reveal His plan step by step. Only He knew the perfect timing, and it would seem a long time—generations and generations—before Jesus Christ came to bring salvation. Did God have any provision for sin until that time would come? Yes, He did.

Until Christ came to make an end of sins, God provided that an innocent lamb or kid goat could be killed as a substitute to cover man's sin. The innocent died for the guilty. Hebrews 9:22 makes it clear that without the shedding of blood there is no forgiveness for sin. Although the blood of an animal could not actually take away sin, it was accepted as a covering until Christ could complete the work Himself. By providing for a substitute death, God could be just and man could be forgiven.

From the very beginning even until now, sacrifice is a common practice in many parts of the world. Something within the human heart tells us that we need to do something because of our sin. But many are very ignorant of the right way to find forgiveness. The Bible is the only guide that can point us to Jesus, who is *"the way, the truth, and the life"* (John 14:6).

The Bible does not tell us how God instructed Adam or his sons about sacrifice. But the fact that God made coats of skin to cover the naked bodies of Adam and Eve implies that some animals were killed to provide those coverings. It may be that the death of those animals and their blood was a sacrifice to cover Adam and Eve's sin as well. Each time an Old Testament saint offered a lamb for a sin offering, it was a reminder of God's promise of a coming Redeemer.

While God provided that innocent animals could die for the sins of mankind, the sacrifice alone was not sufficient. Even as God required obedience with Adam at the beginning, so obedience must follow sacrifice in order to please God. God does not accept sacrifice without faith expressed by obedience.

After Jesus came, the animal sacrifices of the first covenant were no longer needed. As God's own Son, He offered Himself as a perfect sacrifice:

> *9Then said he, Lo, I come to do thy will, O God. He taketh away the first [covenant], that he may establish the second. 10By the which will we are sanctified through the offering of the body of Jesus Christ once for all.* (Hebrews 10)

No one needs to go through life with a burden of sin. Because of God's boundless mercy, we can find forgiveness and restoration by repenting and placing our faith in the Lord Jesus Christ. He loves each of us more than we can imagine, saying:

> [28]Come unto me, all ye that labour and are heavy laden, and I will give you rest. [29]Take my yoke upon you, and learn of me; for I am meek and lowly in heart: and ye shall find rest unto your souls. [30]For my yoke is easy, and my burden is light. (Matthew 11)

> [20]Now then we are ambassadors for Christ, as though God did beseech you by us: we pray you in Christ's stead, be ye reconciled to God. [21]For he hath made him to be sin for us, who knew no sin; that we might be made the righteousness of God in him. (2 Corinthians 5)

Rejecting God's Way

God's plan for restoring mankind is a wonderful expression of His mercy. But God still gives each person the freedom of choice. We can choose either to receive God's plan or reject it. But choices have consequences. We will soon see how this affected the lives of Adam's children.

The Bible mentions that Adam and Eve had several sons and daughters, perhaps quite a large family, but there were two sons that are especially remembered— Cain and Abel. Let us read why:

> *2...And Abel was a keeper of sheep, but Cain was a tiller of the ground.*
>
> *3And in process of time it came to pass, that Cain brought of the fruit of the ground an offering unto the Lord. 4And Abel, he also brought of the firstlings of his flock and of the fat thereof. And the Lord had respect unto Abel and to his offering: 5But unto Cain and to his offering he had not respect. And Cain was very wroth, and his countenance fell.*

The difference in the offerings was that Cain brought of the fruit of the ground, while Abel brought an animal sacrifice. *"By faith Abel offered unto God a more excellent sacrifice than Cain, by which he obtained witness that he was righteous, God testifying of his gifts: and by it he being dead yet speaketh"* (Hebrews 11:4). Yes, Cain brought a sacrifice, but not the kind God required (vs. 22). Today people still want to worship God in their own way. But if we want the blessing of God on our lives, we must be careful to follow God's directions like Abel did. God does not accept alternatives, even if they seem "just as good" to us.

God would not accept Cain on Cain's terms, and Cain got mad.

> ⁶*And the Lord said unto Cain, Why art thou wroth? and why is thy countenance fallen? ⁷If thou doest well, shalt thou not be accepted? and if thou doest not well, sin lieth at the door. And unto thee shall be his desire, and thou shalt rule over him.*

These are some very important questions to consider. But the Bible doesn't tell us how Cain responded right then, or how much he thought about God's warning. Just like with Adam and Eve, God made it clear to Cain how he could be accepted. So why would anyone reject God's way and fight back? The account we are reading shows how sin works when Satan is in control, causing people to go farther and farther from God. When we reject God's counsel, sin is truly at our door, ready to pounce on us. If we do not *"rule over him,"* we will certainly be attacked. It worked that way for Cain and it will for us too. What drives our heart feelings? God understands us better than we understand ourselves. It is always better to heed His warning and follow His way than to take our own.

> ⁸*And Cain talked with Abel his brother: and it came to pass, when they were in the field, that Cain rose up against Abel his brother, and slew him.*

Why in the world did Cain kill his very own brother?! The Bible tells us: *"Because his own works were evil, and his brother's righteous"* (1 John 3:12). Maybe Abel encouraged Cain to do what God said, or maybe Cain was angry because Abel was a "goodie goodie." When someone is doing wrong, they get provoked when their conscience pricks them, so they don't like being around those who are doing right, any more than a righteous person enjoys being around those who are being wicked. *"An unjust man is an abomination to the just: and he that is upright in the way is abomination to the wicked"* (Proverbs 29:27). There is always tension between righteousness and wickedness. That is a situation we cannot evade while living in this world. Sinners hate righteousness because it condemns them. Hate turns into murder. *"Whosoever hateth his brother is a murderer: and ye know that no murderer hath eternal life abiding in him"* (1 John 3:15). Cain's example shows us where an evil heart will take us, and why people hate and kill today. It grows from the evil that Satan plants in their hearts.

When conflict arises between people and one mistreats another, often a spirit of revenge is aroused. The one hurt says they want to "get even," but getting even hardly ever happens. Usually they return the mistreatment in greater measure. The Old Testament law restrained that natural inclination of man by controlling the response: *"eye for eye, tooth for tooth"* (Leviticus 24:19-20). When conflicts are allowed to grow, man's worst behavior is revealed.

> 9*And the Lord said unto Cain, Where is Abel thy brother?*
>
> *And he said, I know not: Am I my brother's keeper?*
>
> 10*And he said, What hast thou done? the voice of thy brother's blood crieth unto me from the ground.*

Did you notice the downward course in Cain's life? Self-will and disobedience, hatred, murder, lying, and desertion of duty. When we do what is wrong, we may think that we are in control, but actually we are permitting ourselves to be bound by Satan. Each time someone rejects God, their heart grows harder against Him. And as their conscience gets weaker, evil deeds don't seem quite so bad as they once did.

God had told Cain, *"If thou doest well, shalt thou not be accepted?"* But instead, Cain had killed his brother Abel. How did that help? We reap what we sow, and are judged for what we do. Because of Cain's rebellion, God had to punish Cain:

> *[11]And now art thou cursed from the earth, which hath opened her mouth to receive thy brother's blood from thy hand; [12]When thou tillest the ground, it shall not henceforth yield unto thee her strength; a fugitive and a vagabond shalt thou be in the earth.*
>
> *[13]And Cain said unto the Lord, My punishment is greater than I can bear....*
>
> *[16]And Cain went out from the presence of the Lord, and dwelt in the land of Nod, on the east of Eden.*

Turning away from any thought of repentance, it seems that Cain's only response was to complain about his punishments. Sin causes hard hearts, and one disappointment after another. God will allow us to reject Him, but we cannot escape the consequences.

Cain's Ungodly Posterity

As long as life continues, consequences continue as well. When we do wrong, not only does it affect us and those immediately around us, but it also lays the groundwork for the same sins to grow in our children. In fact, when God was warning the Israelites against idolatry, He said, *"I the Lord thy God am a jealous God, visiting the iniquity of the fathers upon the children unto the third and fourth generation of them that hate me"* (Exodus 20:5). So what do you expect happened in Cain's family and the families of others who rejected God? We will soon see.

As you recall, mankind had been created in the image of God. As a result, the first people were extremely intelligent and creative, not some sort of ignorant cave men. The thing that marred that marvelous wisdom and knowledge was the evil in their hearts because of sin. After Cain's rebellion against God, his children followed in his footsteps. Evil continued to fill their minds, and all his descendents became very corrupt. But they still were very worldly wise.

While Genesis does not tell us how long Cain and his descendents lived, it appears that before the Flood most people lived very long lives. The overlapping generations would have allowed knowledge and inventions to increase rapidly. And because of their long lives the population on the earth would have increased very rapidly. Genesis 4:17 tells us that Cain built a city, which he named after his son Enoch. Perhaps the townspeople included many of his other descendants, as well as the descendants of his brothers and sisters that are not named in the Bible.

Genesis 4 gives us some insight to their activity. We know that at first Cain had been a farmer like his father. And we also learn the occupations of some of his descendants of the sixth generation:

²⁰And Adah bare Jabal: he was the father of such as dwell in tents, and of such as have cattle. ²¹And his brother's name was Jubal: he was the father of all such as handle the harp and organ. ²²And Zillah, she also bare Tubal-cain, an instructer of every artificer in brass and iron: and the sister of Tubal-cain was Naamah.

Here we find notable progress in animal husbandry, music, and smithing. The people before the flood were certainly experienced in industry and art. Although the Bible doesn't give us a timeline of these developments, it is likely that Adam was still living at this time.

But along with progress in knowledge came further decline in morality. The Adah and Zillah mentioned above were both wives of a man named Lamech. Not only did this man break God's design for a single couple in marriage, but he is also on record for murder, which he justified just like Cain had (4:23-24). Things only got worse in the generations following, and the sixth chapter of Genesis gives us a picture that is a sorry sight indeed:

¹And it came to pass, when men began to multiply on the face of the earth, and daughters were born unto them, ²That the sons of God saw the daughters of men that they were fair; and they took them wives of all which they chose.

³And the Lord said, My spirit shall not always strive with man, for that he also is flesh: yet his days shall be an hundred and twenty years.

⁴There were giants in the earth in those days; and also after that, when the sons of God came in unto the daughters of men, and they bare children to them, the same became mighty men which were of old, men of renown.

There are different ideas of who the *"sons of God"* were, but it is the opinion of this author that they were children of the godly line of Seth who married the descendents of Cain. When the righteous marry the unrighteous we can expect the same results as the people described above—worldly wise, but evil at heart.

> *5And God saw that the wickedness of man was great in the earth, and that every imagination of the thoughts of his heart was only evil continually. 6And it repented the Lord that he had made man on the earth, and it grieved him at his heart. 7And the Lord said, I will destroy man whom I have created from the face of the earth; both man, and beast, and the creeping thing, and the fowls of the air; for it repenteth me that I have made them....*
> *11The earth also was corrupt before God, and the earth was filled with violence. 12And God looked upon the earth, and, behold, it was corrupt; for all flesh had corrupted his way upon the earth.*

Wickedness, evil imaginations, corruption, and violence. What a terrible world they created for themselves! Multitudes suffered because of Cain's rebellion against God.

These verses also reveal the heart of God. We can see that God in His mercy would not allow their wicked lives to continue. Sin must be punished and brought to an end. The 120 years was likely the lead time of mercy given before God took them all away in the Great Flood. God allows each man to choose his own way, but in the end each must face the results of the life he has lived. In many cases, God leaves the door of mercy open a long time. But that should only move us to repent while we may, for there will come a day for each of us when it will be too late. *"For God shall bring every work into judgment, with every secret thing, whether it be good, or whether it be evil"* (Ecclesiastes 12:14).

The choices we are making today may seem very small and unnoticed. But each choice is a step forward on our journey. A journey on the path of blessing or of cursing. A journey that affects the lives of all who follow us. And God is watching each choice we make. *"For the eyes of the Lord are over the righteous, and his ears are open unto their prayers: but the face of the Lord is against them that do evil"* (1 Peter 3:12).

Seth's Godly Lineage

> ²⁵*And Adam knew his wife again; and she bare a son, and called his name Seth: For God, said she, hath appointed me another seed instead of Abel, whom Cain slew.*

When Cain was born, Eve had said, "*I have gotten a man from the Lord*" (Genesis 4:1). She was evidently hoping he was the promised seed—the Deliverer who would bruise Satan. Oh, how bitter must have been her disappointment when Cain instead murdered Abel and fled from God. The path he chose wrecked the hopes she had for both boys. So when she gave birth to another son, Eve was comforted that God was supplying a replacement, and hope revived. No matter how discouraging our circumstances may appear, God is never discouraged. He always has a way of fulfilling His promises.

> ²⁶*And to Seth, to him also there was born a son; and he called his name Enos: then began men to call upon the name of the Lord.*

Seth gave his son a name that means "mortal." As he observed the lives of those around him, he recognized the fact that we humans are frail creatures. Even at our best, we cannot solve the problems we help create. Up until this time it appears that God was the one that called upon men, but now, seeing their need of God, men began to call upon Him. Let us be wise as well. The only way we can live a godly life is to recognize our great need, and respond to God's call by calling upon Him for help.

Genesis chapter 5 gives us a record of the lineage from Adam through Seth over the generations to Noah's time. Since it includes their ages, this important record helps us form a timeline from Creation to the Flood. Only the direct line of descent is named, but most of these men lived hundreds of years, *"and begat sons and daughters."* God had intended man to multiply and fill the earth (Genesis 1:28), and no doubt a population explosion developed as each generation enlarged the family circle.

Of course, as we learned in the last lesson, that whole human family was far from the happy company they could have been. If you take the time to study the names of these men, you will find hints of what was going on at the time. But let us jump down the list to the seventh generation, where we find the unique account of Enoch:

> ²¹*And Enoch lived sixty and five years, and begat Methuselah:* ²²*And Enoch walked with God after he begat Methuselah three hundred years, and begat sons and daughters:* ²³*And all the days of Enoch were three hundred sixty and five years:* ²⁴*And Enoch walked with God: and he was not; for God took him.*

Cain walked away from God, but Enoch walked with God. As the world around him was reveling in wickedness, he chose to seek what would please God, instead of pleasing himself. That was no easy path, and he must have endured much mocking and persecution in his pilgrimage. But as he sought God, God answered, and His reality filled Enoch's life. Enoch's relationship to God was so close and precious that God chose to take him from this world without having to die.

We too may walk with God. It doesn't seem at all natural to those who don't know God, but because He wants us, He gives us the key: *"And ye shall seek me, and find me, when ye shall search for me with all your heart"* (Jeremiah 29:13). If we faithfully walk with God here, as

Enoch did, death will be but the door to a much more wonderful life with Him in heaven. And though we leave it to God to decide what manner of death will glorify Him, if we are among the faithful remnant still alive at His coming, we too will be welcomed into His presence without dying.

At the end of the lineage in Genesis 5 we are introduced to another man who was outstanding in his generation. Noah (whose name means "rest") would not have known his great-grandfather Enoch, for he was born many years after God took Enoch away. But the light of faith had not gone out in the earth, for Noah walked with God as Enoch had. He also had many difficult things to face in life, because of the evil being continually done by sinners all around him. As you recall from our earlier reading in Genesis 6, things had gotten so bad that God had decided to bring judgment on the world.

> [8]*But Noah found grace in the eyes of the Lord.*
> [9]*These are the generations of Noah: Noah was a just man and perfect in his generations, and Noah walked with God.* [10]*And Noah begat three sons, Shem, Ham, and Japheth....*
>
> [13]*And God said unto Noah, The end of all flesh is come before me; for the earth is filled with violence through them; and, behold, I will destroy them with the earth.* [14]*Make thee an ark of gopher wood; rooms shalt thou make in the ark, and shalt pitch it within and without with pitch....*
>
> [17]*And, behold, I, even I, do bring a flood of waters upon the earth, to destroy all flesh, wherein is the breath of life, from under heaven; and every thing that is in the earth shall die.* [18]*But with thee will I establish my covenant; and thou shalt come into the ark,*

thou, and thy sons, and thy wife, and thy sons'
wives with thee....
  ²²*Thus did Noah; according to all that God*
commanded him, so did he.

Walking with God may mean that all other friendships must be cut off. But being a friend of God and finding grace in His eyes is worth everything. Because God saw that Noah was *"perfect in his generations,"* God made a covenant to save him and his family from the coming judgment.

This is the first record of God making a covenant with man. When God makes a covenant, He always sets the terms. He told Noah what He was promising, and what Noah should do. God always keeps His part of the agreement. Our part must be to respond with obedience. And that's what Noah did. *"According to all that God commanded him, so did he."*

Noah set an example for all time on how men should respond to God. In the New Testament, God reveals the new covenant He has made for us now. The Bible says it is *"a better covenant, which was established upon better promises"* (Hebrews 8:6). What are the better promises? *"I will put my laws into their hearts, and in their minds will I write them; And their sins and iniquities will I remember no more"* (Hebrews 10:16-17). This is the covenant paid for on the cross by Jesus, who came to save His people from their sins. As we respond properly to God by truly receiving His Son Jesus, God fulfills His part of the covenant, giving us *"power to become the sons of God"* (John 1:12).

But if we reject God's terms, and follow our own selfish ways, we will end up like the wicked and unbelieving in Noah's day, who perished in the Flood. God gave them many opportunities to repent, and Noah preached to them faithfully while the ark was being built. But in the end, only eight people climbed aboard.

Just think—only eight! In each of the passing generations since the Fall of Man, there had been some who responded to God with a heart to walk with Him. But that choice is one each must make for themselves. No matter how much those faithful men may have taught their children to fear and obey God, each child had to choose on his own the path he would take. Of the many sons and daughters that were born, the evidence indicates that most of the children, even those with godly parents, were drawn to the ungodly society about them, and they became companions of ungodly people. The Bible gives us this solemn warning: *"Know ye not that the friendship of the world is enmity with God? whosoever therefore will be a friend of the world is the enemy of God"* (James 4:4).

The Bible doesn't describe much about what it was like on that day so long ago when Noah and his family climbed aboard the ark for keeps. For them, it was just one more step on their journey of obedience. Yet it most likely felt like a momentous step indeed. Can you imagine all the thoughts and emotions that filled each of them that day? Memories of what they were leaving behind. Wondering what lay ahead on their journey. And, most importantly, renewing their decision to obey God. Perhaps Noah gave one more invitation to the worldly people to come join them and be saved. Perhaps the enemies of God mocked them once more for what seemed such a foolish choice. But when God shut the door, and the Flood was released upon the world, it soon became apparent to all who were the ones that had chosen foolishly, and who had chosen wisely.

You in Your World Today

Thank you for joining me in taking this journey into reality. In this book we have tried to look at life from the vantage point of God's revelation to us in the Bible. God's revelation helps us to understand:
- when and how the world began
- why you and I are alive
- why bad things happen
- what happens after we die
- how to find true peace with God

In short, God's revelation helps us to know the truth, which is reality.

But we don't have to look at life this way. We can choose to ignore God's revelation, and decide that we just have to figure everything out for ourselves. Many are doing that. Many have decided not to believe the Bible, and instead have put their trust in "smart" scientists, who come up with other ideas about where the world came from, and all of us, too. From that world view, things simply cannot be the way the Bible says. And it all looks logical to those who leave God out of the picture.

And yet, in spite of all the thinking and reasoning of "smart" people, reality is still there. It cannot be changed to accommodate men's ideas. It is true that scientists can learn many things, and especially over the past couple hundred years they have invented many tools for life and for understanding how the world works. But in spite of all this "progress," there are still as many problems in the world as ever, because scientists have not found a way to fix selfishness and sin, and they reject God's way. We will never find God or Satan by looking through a telescope, and no science experiment will explain sin in the human heart. Science cannot tell us what happened in the beginning, and it cannot show us what will happen after we die.

As we have started reading through the Bible, we have found the stories of people just like you and me. People that wake up in the morning and have work to do. People that rub shoulders with others and get on each other's nerves. People that experience life like we all do, and have to answer to God for the choices they make. We have read of Adam and Eve. Of Cain and Abel. Of Lamech and Enoch. Keep reading through the rest of the Bible, and you will find a whole host of people to learn from. Those who chose wisely, and those who didn't. Those who fell for Satan's lies, and those who valued truth.

And now it's your turn. Your choices are the ones that will determine your destiny—for life as well as eternity.

> ¹³*Let us hear the conclusion of the whole matter: Fear God, and keep his commandments: for this is the whole duty of man.* ¹⁴*For God shall bring every work into judgment, with every secret thing, whether it be good, or whether it be evil.* (Ecclesiastes 12)

> ¹²*And, behold, I come quickly; and my reward is with me, to give every man according as his work shall be....*
> ¹⁴*Blessed are they that do his commandments, that they may have right to the tree of life, and may enter in through the gates into the city.* (Revelation 22)

That is reality.

CPSIA information can be obtained
at www.ICGtesting.com
Printed in the USA
FSOW04n1224070515
6911FS